Mastering Business Development®

7422 Carmel Executive Park Drive
Suite 202
Charlotte, NC 28226
Phone: (704) 553-0000
Fax: (704) 553-0001
www.mbdi.com

Winning Conversations: Mastering the Art of Business Development
Second Edition | December 2010
ISBN-13: 978-1-456-349752
ISBN-10: 14563497959

Copyright © 1998-2010. Published by Mastering Business Development, Inc. (MBDi)
7422 Carmel Executive Park Drive, Suite 202
Charlotte, NC 28226
(704) 553-0000, (800) 553-7944 | FAX (704) 553-0001
Internet: http://www.mbdi.com

Contents

1

First Things First

Welcome to MBD's Mastering Business Development, a basic program developed for the experienced and senior-level Business Development Professional. As you begin your course in Professional Business Development, let's first talk about why you are here. Why has your company decided to ask you to participate in this training, and what do you hope to gain from it?

As a senior-level professional working in Business Development, you are one of your company's most valuable resources. You have a thorough knowledge of the technical aspects of your company's product or service. You also have developed a seasoned understanding of both the marketplace in which your company operates and your customer base.

However, your company's management senses a need for change. Like more and more companies in today's competitive marketplace, they realize their company cannot succeed with a passive and reactive sales team. Instead, they need a highly trained and proactive team of Business Development Professionals. They realize they need to evolve to a level at which they know what business to pursue and they have a systematic approach to developing it. They need people who have the skills, ability, and thinking to function effectively in the role of Business Development. These individuals need to have their own system, rather than being part of someone else's, or the marketplace's, system.

You are being asked to accept the additional challenge of Professional Business Development as part of your position. Your company realizes that you need to acquire a basis of helpful concepts and specific techniques to enhance your opportunities to succeed in this expanded role. That's why you have been selected to participate in this course. Because of your position, your special talents and your ability, you are seen as someone with the potential to help move your company to the level of proactive Business Development. Oftentimes there are people who have an interest, a desire, and the ability to go after new business, but have not seriously considered doing so. With the proper training and development, they could function well in the role of Business Development. Your management senses that you are such an individual.

A comprehensive training process like this can help you understand what Business Development in the 21st century is all about and what is necessary for success in a professional product or services business such as yours. Our goal is to give people like you – professionals with technical knowledge – enough information on Professional Business Development that you can decide for yourself if you want to take on this all-important role.

When we're finished, you will be able to decide if you want to enter the world of Professional Business Development, and, if so, at what level. You may want to devote 10 percent, 50 percent or 100 percent of your time to this endeavor. You may even want to lead and manage the process for your company. You'll have sufficient information to make a free and informed choice as to whether – and to what extent – you want to get involved in this role. We'll help you identify whether you have the talent, the willingness, and the mind-set to be successful at Professional Business Development.

You'll find out what is necessary to learn in order to be reasonably intelligent in the area of Professional Business Development. It will get you in the door.

It won't make you proficient, but it will give you an objective perspective of what Business Development is all about so you can decide whether or not you want to choose this role for yourself.

What you won't find in this course or any of our material is any mention of the tricks and gimmicks of traditional selling – the kind of "grab 'em by the tie and choke 'em 'til they buy" techniques that make up so much of traditional selling behavior.

Rather, we will concentrate on the more elemental questions. We'll talk about why people buy, instead of how to sell. We'll talk about your self-concept and how limiting self-perceptions may hinder your success in Professional Business Development. We'll talk about a few solid techniques that work and how to apply these techniques within a process. We'll talk, in short, about tested principles that produce results.

The senior-level prospects and clients on whom you call expect to be approached in a professional manner by serious, thoughtful, top-level executives. In Mastering Business Development you will learn exactly how to contact these important prospects in the manner and at the level of thinking that works.

Ultimately, your decision whether to become involved in Professional Business Development will be up to you. But remember this: No matter how much or how little of your time you decide to devote to this role, you must give 100 percent of your effort during that time.

> *No matter how much or how little of your time you decide to devote to this role, you must give 100 percent of your effort during that time.*

The short-term goal of this training process is to acquaint you with Professional Business Development so you can decide if it is an area in which you want to test your capabilities. The long-term goal is strikingly ambitious. We will make you so good in Business Development that you will seriously consider leaving your organization and doing it on your own. Our goal is to create "intrapreneurs"– entrepreneurs within the company. If you find you like Business Development so much and feel so proficient at it that you think more than once about resigning and starting your own Business Development firm, then we've succeeded.

Develop and use your own system, or you will become part of someone else's system.

Of course, we're not seriously trying to get you to leave your company. But we are trying to move you to a position of strength with regard to Business Development – a position where you know exactly what business is worth going after, how to secure it, and why it is good for you and your organization. Then, if you find your goals for Business Development and those of your company are congruent, you can make a conscious decision to use your skills there.

So let's get on with it. Let's first look at a few fundamental principles for success in Professional Business Development.

■ Develop and use your own system, or you will become part of someone else's system.

■ You must learn and use a system of proactive prospecting, lead tracking and Business Development. Any system will work as long as you use it. But you must be aware of what you are doing and implement a system. Otherwise you will become part of your client's or your competitor's system.

■ Think like a business person, not a salesperson. There is a significant difference. You want to operate from the mental perspective of a business professional conducting business on a long-term, win-win basis, not just in a buy-sell situation.

4

What do we mean by this? Here's an example:

In a challenging economy, proactive people who know Professional Business Development have no immediate concerns. Their competition, which has been reactive to the marketplace, is huddling up and wondering what to do. The truth is, in a challenging economy there still exists about 80 percent of the business that was ever available. Those who know Professional Business Development continue to feast. They cruise right along, independent of the marketplace or the product or the company or other external forces. They don't externalize control over their situation, convincing themselves that external factors make the difference between success and failure. They internalize control. They realize the truth of the old saying, "If it is to be, it's up to me." They claim responsibility for the position they're in, realizing it is the result of what they've chosen to do or not to do in the past. They have helped create the situation they're in, and they take responsibility for working in it. If they see a slowdown coming, they begin immediately to bring about the transition from reactive order taking to proactive Business Development. They realize there is always enough business for a good company to be successful. It's just a matter of knowing how to go after it proactively.

> *You must learn and use a system of proactive prospecting, lead tracking and Business Development.*

> *Think like a business person, not a salesperson.*

Now some of this may sound foreign to you. If so, we must caution you to resist the common human tendency to take new information and fit it into your present belief system and traditional ways of operating within your company. Be warned: You may have to throw out much of what you've learned before. To be successful, you have to adopt new ways of looking at Business Development, totally new ways of operating. If you are successful, your company will be successful. And we, as your Business Development consultants, will be successful. That's why we cannot allow you to limit your ability to be successful by remaining loyal to the philosophy or history of your past. The definition of insanity is to keep doing what you've always done, expecting different results.

What you will glean from this overview is a better picture of what you need to learn. You may find out how ignorant you are in areas that critically affect your financial well-being. We will lay out for you what is necessary to learn in order to succeed in Professional Business Development, which is quite different from traditional sales and marketing. If you choose to enter this arena, be prepared to pay the price. To be successful, you must be prepared to pay full price one time. Nothing short of your best effort will succeed.

You will learn a number of valuable rules. One is: There's a limit to how smart you can be, but there is no limit to how dumb you can be. When you feel ignorant, that's when you begin to learn. When you realize that you don't know everything, you are taking the first step down the road to success.

Consider, for example, a group of professionals who are in pain because they see business opportunities being missed. That's an ideal group to learn and apply very quickly the lessons of Professional Business Development. When the pain of change is less than the pain you're in, you will pay the price of change. There is no growth without pain.

If you decide to pursue this course in Professional Business Development, you'll learn to understand and manage four important issues:

- Technical Issues
- Money Issues
- Business Issues
- People Issues

Of these, people issues are by far the most important and the most difficult. As you strive to become a Business Development Professional, you will encounter both mechanical and conceptual limitations. Mechanical limitations will affect your ability to execute a Business Development process. These are limitations of skill, information, and base process.

Far more important, and far more difficult, are conceptual limitations. These are limitations that affect your ability to manage people and behavior – and most importantly, your ability to manage your own behavior.

Learning Professional Business Development is not all that hard. We can teach you everything there is to learn about the process, systems and skills of Business Development in a matter of days. But it will take more than a year for you to understand why you will struggle doing many of the things you are taught to do. Dealing with your own conceptual limitations, the emotional limitations you bring with you to the role of Business Development, is the most challenging hurdle you will face.

If you decide to pursue your interest in Professional Business Development, you will learn to face and clear this hurdle. And in clearing it you'll find that the key to success on a fundamental, personal level is in fact the key to success in Business Development as well.

2

The Twelve Core Competencies of Professional Business Development

Why Traditional Sales Thinking Fails

For every nine individuals who enter the role of Business Development, six will fail within a year. Of the remaining three, two will eventually make approximately $40,000 a year in the role. And only one of the original nine will ever make it long-term as a Professional. Why?

Documented surveys consistently reveal that traditional salespeople fail in 90 percent of their calls.

Research shows that 80 percent of the business people who are not engaged in Business Development are better qualified to be doing it than are 50 percent of the people who are doing it. In fact, 50 percent of the people in the Business Development profession today should not be employed there. Of the remaining 50 percent, half should not be representing the product they are selling. They are ill-suited – by temperament or training – to be associated with their chosen product line.

Despite the large sums of money most companies invest in traditional sales training programs and meetings every year, the results of their efforts are not encouraging. Documented surveys consistently reveal that traditional salespeople fail in 90 percent of their calls. Recent surveys of 10,000 buyers found these disturbing statistics:

■ 81 percent of them could not recall the name of their salesperson one year after their purchase because of lack of follow-up.

- 63 percent said they would not buy from the same salesperson or company again and cited "neglect" and "indifference" as the reasons.

- 85 percent said the salesperson lacked empathy or ability to understand their problem.

- 96 percent said the salesperson didn't ask for a commitment because he or she apparently "lost control" of the situation.

- 88 percent said the salesperson did not present the products and services he or she was selling, but appeared to be selling price instead of product benefits or solutions.

- 89 percent said the salesperson did not understand the product he or she was representing.

If these are the results of all the money and effort American businesses expend to train traditional salespeople in traditional sales thinking, then apparently this type of training is not the answer.

Confirming evidence of this problem is found in a 10-year study of more than 18,000 salespeople by the Caliper Human Strategies organization, which found that part of the answer lies in proper selection and placement of sales and Business Development Professionals:

The Caliper studies show that 55 percent of the people earning their living in sales should be doing something else. Quite simply, they do not have the personality attributes to succeed in sales. Another 20 to 25 percent have what it takes to sell, but they should be selling a different product. These individuals could be successful in some selling situations, but are only marginal in their current sales position. This leaves approximately 20 percent of salespeople who genuinely possess the personality attributes needed to succeed in selling and are selling the products or services best suited to their personalities. The same studies indicate that this 20 percent of properly placed people are precisely the same individuals responsible for selling 80 percent of what is sold.

Traditional Sales Thinking vs. Business Development Thinking

One reason so many traditional salespeople are ineffective is that they are following an outmoded, ineffective method of selling. They are slaves to traditional, old-fashioned selling techniques and traditional thinking that make their prospects bristle the minute they begin a sales call.

One reason so many traditional salespeople are ineffective is that they are following an outmoded, ineffective method of selling.

Traditional salespeople fit all the stereotypes. They are like vultures, ever poised and ready to pounce upon the unsuspecting prospect at the first sign of weakness, which they are trained to interpret as a "buying signal."

Their behavior is the natural outgrowth of the type of training and supervision they have received in traditional selling organizations. Most often, they have been taught ideas like these:

■ Selling is a numbers game. You win by presenting the features and benefits of your goods to enough people. Some of them are certain to buy.

■ Aggressiveness is a virtue that must be cultivated and frequently used.

■ Most prospects don't buy. They must be "sold."

■ Sales is a competitive game, and you need to experience the thrill of the sale.

- The "close" is the climax and focal point of the sale. Everything else is just a prelude to getting the prospect's name on the dotted line.

Within seconds after the initial contact with a prospect, the difference between the traditional salesperson and a Professional in Business Development is evident. When a prospective client encounters the traditional approach, he or she thinks, "Oh, my God. It's another high-pressure salesperson out to sell me something. I'm going to have to sit through another dog and pony show, and then there will be a heavy close. I had better be wary."

A better way of comparing the difference in thinking and behavior of the traditional salesperson and the Business Development Professional is to think of the "pro," the Professional, and the "con," the traditional vulture-like seller. Since the prospect often feels he or she is being "conned," the epithet is well chosen. Here are a few examples:

- The traditional salesperson, the con, sees selling as an event, and the close as the event's focal point. Just look at the number of books and training programs on traditional selling, with their emphasis on closing techniques and handling prospects' stalls and objections. The Business Development Professional knows that the close of the business agreement is nothing more than the natural conclusion to a well-executed communication process.

The close of the business agreement is nothing more than the natural conclusion to a well-executed communication process.

- The traditional salesperson, the con, is self-centered and operates from a position of scarcity. His or her major question is "What's in it for me?" The Business Development Professional is client-focused. He or she gets inside the business and the mind of the prospect and sees the situation from the client's perspective.

■ The con sees the client as a disposable commodity to be used, abused and discarded, if necessary, to move his or her products or services. The con believes it is easier to find a new prospect than build a relationship. The Professional in Business Development sees the client as an integral part of a long-term, mutually beneficial and profitable relationship.

The Business Development Professional is client-focused and sees the situation from the client's perspective.

■ The con thinks all prospects will buy eventually, and he or she is prepared to endure the fight. The con interprets a "no" as failure, quite often taking it personally and professionally. The Business Development Professional realizes that only qualified prospects buy and do so for their own reasons. He understands that the most effective use of his time and skills is to allow prospects to disqualify themselves and then move on.

The traditional salesperson is confrontational. She always tries to push the prospect to buy. The Business Development Professional knows it's more important to help prospects identify their concerns, decide whether or not they want to do something about them and help them seek a solution. The Professional helps prospects do what is in their best interest, short-term and long-term.

The Professional in Business Development sees the client as an integral part of a long-term, mutually beneficial and profitable relationship.

Translating Leads Into Revenue

In our workshops, we frequently ask our clients in Business Development to consider this scenario: "Assume you give your best people charged with Business Development 10 prospective clients. These 10 prospective clients are the types who are most likely to need your company's product or service. How many of the 10 would you expect your best people to produce business with?"

Sadly, the most frequent response is "No more than three."

It follows, then, that if the most skilled, experienced and focused Professionals can only produce revenue with three out of 10 prospects, no salesperson should expect to be able to sell to all 10 people he or she talks to. Obviously, the real skill in developing business is not in identifying and selling the three who are going to buy. The <u>real skill is in quickly identifying the seven who won't.</u>

The Professional helps prospects do what is in their best interest, short-term and long-term.

Top Business Development Professionals have the ability to identify quickly those prospects who are not qualified for their product or service and to leave gracefully and professionally. These Professionals see themselves making just as much money for their company and as great a contribution to the process by identifying non-prospects as by selling to a qualified prospective client. They know that the better their skills in identifying non-buyers, the better is their pool of legitimate prospects, and therefore the better are their revenue results.

The traditional salesperson will keep trying to push until a sale happens. The Business Development Professional has learned to tell himself, "Seven of these 10 people do not have issues or pains requiring my solution. The quicker I determine that, the more effective I will be." The traditional salesperson will instead be thinking, "What could I have done to sell that person who refused today?"

The role of the Professional Business Development person is much like that of the physician. Can you imagine a cardiovascular surgeon, for example, going home in the evening frustrated after examining a 25-year-old professional football player and finding him absolutely healthy? Of course not. The physician's concern is focused on the thoroughness of the examination, not the prospects for surgery. If the exam turns up a healthy patient, it is still successful. The same is true for Professional Business Development people.

Another indicator of the traditional sales approach vs. Professional Business Development is in the way the salesperson conducts an interview. Traditional salespeople spend:

■ About 5 percent of their time in qualifying.

■ About 15 percent of their time looking for problems.

■ About 35 percent of their time presenting features and benefits.

■ Almost half their time handling stalls and objections from the prospect – believing whoever gives up first loses.

The Professional in Business Development, on the other hand, invests:

⊙ About 50 percent of their time in diagnosing and identifying the problems, if in fact they exist.

⊙ About 35 percent of their time in designing the solution.

⊙ About 10 percent of their time in a specific presentation.

⊙ Less than 5 percent of their time in concluding the business agreement, which by this time is amicable to both parties.

Like a good physician, the Professional in Business Development wants to know not only where it hurts, but also why there is a pain. He or she does not prescribe a cure until the root of the illness has been discovered and understood.

Three Classes of Salespeople

Our research indicates there are three distinct classes of traditional sales-people: the Pest, the Peddler and the Professional Salesperson. The first two follow the traditional sales approach, which we have just described. The last approaches his or her work from a less traditional sales approach, somewhat similar to that of a Business Development Professional. If you are a manager in Business Development, it is helpful for you to know how to classify your people and help them move up the ladder of Professionalism.

- The Pest – The pest has limited knowledge of the prospects, the industry, the products and the profession. Pests also have little, if any, traditional sales skills. They simply go places and talk to anyone who breathes, generally making themselves a bother. Pests' main focus is to keep busy, so they spend a lot of time planning calls and managing activities. They fail to understand that activity is not accomplishment and energy is not work. Because pests are so common, many prospective clients see most traditional salespeople in this light.

While "management by wandering around" is quite an effective technique, sales by wandering around produces significantly less meaningful results. It is not Professional sales or Professional Business Development. Pests stumble into business by participating in what might be called unorganized accidents. If you drive a car where other cars are, for example, sooner or later you will be involved in an accident. The trouble is, you don't know when.

Pests fail to understand that activity is not accomplishment and energy is not work.

That's how the pest sells. Every so often he will end up getting some business, typically known as a mercy sale. However, the pest can't explain the conditions and can't reproduce the accidental sale with any predictability. Research has shown us that as many as 40 percent of people in sales can be classified as pests.

- The Peddler – The peddler reflects every stereotype of salespeople. Peddlers see their job as "moving stuff." Their idea of a complete needs analysis is, "What do you need?" Followed by an explanation that, if they don't have it, you probably don't need it. Peddlers are individuals who bring and brag, tell and sell. Their morning motivational chant is, "grab 'em by the tie and choke 'em 'til they buy."

No question about it, peddlers know what they are doing. They have studied a lot of processes carefully and have come to believe that most sales occur during or shortly after the presentation. For this reason, they make lots of free presentations to unqualified prospects. They learn that following any good presentation, you should ask for the order, so they spend a lot of time asking for the order. They also have been incorrectly trained to believe that what prevents sales are stalls and objections, so they have practiced and refined the art of overcoming these obstacles. They refine their process down to a fine science that, regrettably, is lacking in both effectiveness and concern for the customer.

As many as 50 percent of people who enter sales progress only to the peddler level. To continue the auto analogy, the peddler's type of selling produces organized accidents. It revolves around a series of deliberate moves designed to inflict a sale on the customer. It's sort of like getting into the car, heading for the freeway during rush hour, and speeding mindlessly onto the highway without looking. You've probably already done the math, and it's shocking: Pests and peddlers together make up almost 90 percent of people in traditional sales.

MBD *insights*

Professional salespeople understand they are in the problem-solving/money-making business.

16

■ The Professional Salesperson – The Professional salesperson is the consultative, diagnostic, problem-solving individual who goes in with definite systems, highly developed skills and Professional discipline. The Professional salesperson is among the top 11 percent, the one out of nine with the most likelihood of making it long-term. Professional salespeople have learned why people buy, and they understand part of their own conceptual limitations. They understand they are in the problem-solving/money-making business. They've learned to ask a lot of questions, diagnose problems and put together a unique solution to solve those specific problems.

Their results are no accident. Rather, Professional salespeople foster a problem-driven, generally customer-oriented trip from outset to destination. They generally exhibit fewer of the traditional sales characteristics, and they have begun the process of learning how to think and act like business people. Only about 8 percent of all "salespeople" can be classified as Professional salespeople.

■ The Professional Business Partner – The Professional Business Partner is the ultimate Business Development Professional. He or she is what you want your individuals to become. Professional Business Partners go beyond problem-solving to a focus on problem prevention. They make an effort to build a long-term business relationship with each customer. They transcend the role of consultant and problem-solver to become colleague and partner in their customer's business. They are extremely customer-focused, working from the prospect's perspective. They have learned to balance their own individual goals in Business Development with their purpose, which is to help prospects get their needs met. They help prospects qualify themselves by helping them identify their concerns and helping them to determine whether or not those problems require a solution. They have learned to think like a business person and not like a salesperson.

With the Professional Business Partner, revenue generation is no accident. Think of a Mercedes-Benz engineer attaching sensing devices and cameras to a new Mercedes and then pulling it with a cable down a track at a controlled speed into a brick wall to test the strength of the car's body. The Professional Business Partner uses a procedure this systematized, one that is closely planned and monitored and can be reproduced in exact detail. He or she knows how to make specific modifications that will bring about predictable results. A sale results from a system and a process, not a random accident. Research shows that fewer than 3 percent of all individuals in Business Development can be classified as Professional Business Partners. These are the people you want to become the heart and soul of your Business Development team. They must be carefully identified, promptly selected, properly positioned, and effectively developed.

The Professional Business Partner has learned to think like a business person and not like a salesperson.

What Causes Traditional Salespeople to Fail?

We have pointed out that your goal for your people should be to move them from the traditional sales categories toward becoming Professional Business Partners. To do this, you must know the reasons why they will struggle with the process. What causes them to remain in the lower levels of traditional sales activity and hampers their maturity into top-level Business Development Professionals?

Fewer than 3 percent of all individuals in Business Development can be classified as Professional Business Partners.

Our research has identified three reasons why individuals struggle in this process:

■ Conceptual Problems – These are the problems contained in the six inches between one's ears. They are caused by the emotional limitations that people bring with them to the role of Business Development. They are the outdated, inappropriate attitudes, beliefs, values and feelings – which the individual is unaware of – that limit him or her in this role. This situation can manifest itself in insecurity, immaturity and lack of focus. It is represented when an individual knows what he or she should do, but emotionally or psychologically is uncomfortable in doing it. Conceptual problems represent 60 percent of all the problems individuals have in the role of Business Development. Conceptual problems are not solved by pep talks that pump individuals full of positive mental attitude. They are basic core beliefs and feelings that must be honestly faced and dealt with if the individual is to grow to the next level in his or her profession.

Conceptual problems represent 60 percent of all the problems individuals have in the role of Business Development.

■ Mechanical Problems – Mechanical problems can best be described as a lack of an appropriate prospecting, qualifying and lead-tracking system, along with the related skill knowledge to execute it. Rather than carrying out a Professional Business Development system, traditional salespeople in the lower 89 percent of performance operate from an outdated, traditional system based on features and benefits, "show and tell," and groundless enthusiasm. They repeat the same scenario continually – a scenario that is so mechanical it requires no mental or emotional focus. Any sales process will work to some extent, even though one based on a traditional approach and immature thinking will be very inefficient and ineffective. That's why traditional salespeople get stuck here and never confront the emotional trash that hampers their growth in Business Development. Approximately 30 percent of all the problems people have in sales and Business Development are mechanically based.

Approximately 30 percent of all the problems people have in sales and Business Development are mechanically based.

■ Management Problems – Most individuals in traditional sales have lousy sales managers themselves. They lack goals, plans, self-direction and self-control. With no mental or emotional focus and no Professional system to guide their activity, they get the spotty and inconsistent results one would expect. They expect someone or something external to them to manage them more than they do.

WHY TRADITIONAL SALES THINKING FAILS

Conceptual Problems - 60%
Mechanical Problems - 30%
External Problems - 10%

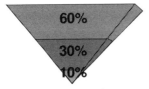

The Problem Is Always Us

These three areas – conceptual, mechanical and self-management – cause many promising Professionals in Business Development to fail. But with honest, energetic commitment from the individual to solve these problems and with an equally energetic commitment on the part of management, they will grow into successful Business Development Professionals. In order to do this, they must learn beyond what has been taught in traditional sales. They must learn to think and act like Business Development Professionals.

The Twelve Core Competencies of Professional Business Development

In our consulting with top technology-oriented companies throughout the country, we've identified 12 core competencies that equip aspiring Professionals to take their place among the top 3 percent of performers in Business Development. We believe that knowledge and its application in these 12 core areas is absolutely necessary to be successful – personally and professionally.

Because they're the most basic requisites, we call the first four of these competencies the Cornerstones of Business Development:

For individuals to be Professional in relationships with their prospects and customers, they must first of all bring to their role a thorough understanding of their product or service. They must master sufficient technical knowledge and its application to understand the problems that they're able to solve for their prospects.

Second, they must bring sufficient business knowledge of their own business and, more importantly, the prospect's business to understand the effects of the solutions they provide for the prospect.

Third, they must bring a thorough understanding of how money is used in business relationships. They must understand how their clients make money and how, by helping clients get their problems solved, they enhance their financial benefit to the prospect.

Fourth, they must have a solid understanding of people's behavior. They must understand why people think and act the way they do, what motivates their prospects to buy and how to relate on a personal basis with the prospects.

The next four competencies of Business Development are usually found in the traditional salesperson. Obviously, they are essential for Business Development Professionals.

First, they must understand personal and Professional goal-setting. This understanding includes goal orientation, the ability to focus on a specific short- or long-term goal and the self-discipline to attain that goal.

Second, they must possess the ability to plan – to figure out the incremental steps necessary to achieve a specific goal. They must know how to be proactive in anticipating obstacles and planning to overcome them as they're encountered.

Third, they must be able to structure their behavior in a productive, proactive process and system in relationships with prospects. They must be able to implement their system, rather than becoming part of the prospect or customer's system.

Fourth, they must refine their interpersonal skills, including the ability to question, listen, nurture, analyze and make decisions.

The last four of our core competencies are clearly characteristics of only the very top echelon of Business Development Professionals. They, more than any other, separate the Professionals in Business Development from the ordinary practitioners. These core competencies include:

First, they understand and have developed principles in Business Development and in life. This entails understanding the core principles that guide them as Professionals—particularly as Professionals in a business relationship with a company or with individuals.

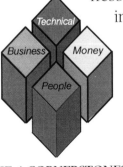

THE 4 CORNERSTONES OF BUSINESS DEVELOPMENT

Second, they understand their mission – not only their mission in life, but also their mission in their role in Business Development. They have identified a collective set of values and principles that constitute their personal mission statement, which guides them in their business relationships with other individuals.

Third, they understand that their purpose in the role of Business Development is to help their clients meet their needs, and they are able to balance this purpose with their own financial goals in Business Development. They understand that in order for them to benefit personally and achieve their financial goals, they must fulfill their purpose by providing benefit to the prospect. They have learned that, in the long run, it is in their best interest to put the purpose of what they do ahead of their own goals.

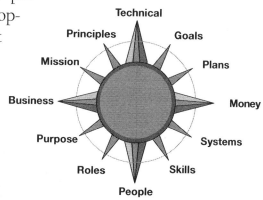

12 CORE COMPETENCIES

Fourth, they have learned to understand the roles that they play in life and to separate these roles from themselves. They know that Business Development is a role and not a venue for value judgment of their worth as individuals.

In the sections that follow, we will look at each of these Twelve Core Competencies and how you can master each one on your journey toward becoming a Professional Business Partner.

3

A Balanced Approach to Personal and Professional Development

We have begun to see that our personal traits exert a considerable influence on our success, or lack of success, in Professional Business Development. One important arena in which it's important to know ourselves is the way we habitually view situations – because of our natural predispositions and, to some extent, because of our culture.

For example, everyone has a natural tendency to look at issues from either a short-term or a long-term perspective. This doesn't mean you can't train yourself to look at problems or opportunities from the opposite view, which is always helpful and sometimes even essential.

It's helpful to know your own predisposition in this area. Then you can forge an approach that is balanced – in both personal and professional development. To attain a point of balance in your thinking, it is necessary to understand the fundamental difference between long-term, strategic thinking and short-term, operational thinking.

Psychologists tell us that thinking comes from two sides of the brain. An oversimplified, but useful, definition of the difference is this: the left brain performs quantitative, measurable, short-term thinking, and the right brain provides intuitive, creative thinking from a long-term perspective. Although most of us haven't done so, we each have the capacity to develop both sides of our brains and to think in both fashions.

Business developers need to balance their right- and left-brain thinking. Our western culture generally has taught us to be more left-brain oriented than right-brain oriented. Therefore, most of us focus more on the quantitative, analytical side of things than we do on the creative side. Most of us have to unlearn this tendency and learn how to let the right-brain, strategic orientation become part of our thinking and guide our behavior.

Characteristics of Left-Brain Thinking

As we see from the graphic at right, the left hemisphere of the brain yields thinking that understands Goals, short-term plans, systems and skills. These short-term and objective elements are necessary ingredients for mastering Business Development. Left-brain thinking is objective thinking that focuses on the quantitative, logical, measurable, and predictive part of our personalities.

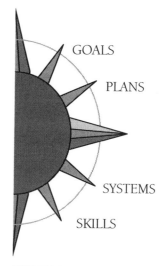

LEFT HEMISPHERE
SHORT-TERM OBJECTIVE

However, while beneficial in many situations, left-brain quantitative thinking tends sometimes to be limited in scope and pragmatic to a fault. When a Business Development Professional has a propensity toward short-term thinking and planning, his capacity to recognize and act upon long-term opportunities is constrained.

For example, recall from Chapter 2 our definition of one's Purpose in Business Development as helping customers meet their needs. It would be difficult to visualize and appreciate one's Purpose using only short-term thinking. Left-brain thinking tends to be more immediately focused than long-term focused. Left-brain-oriented individuals tend to work more on production, rather than on leading and managing. Engaged in Business

Development, they tend to think, "What can I do to get this order?" instead of thinking, "Why do I want this order, and how does this activity fit in with my Purpose, as well as my goal in this role?" They also tend to operate from a position of scarcity, rather than abundance. Because they only understand what can be measured, they believe there is only so much business out there, and they'd better hurry and get their share before it's gone.

Left-brain thinking is objective thinking that focuses on the quantitative, logical, measurable, and predictive part of our personalities.

Just because an individual is naturally oriented toward left-brain thinking, however, is no reason he or she has to accept the limitations imposed by this way of thinking. Though the left-brain thinker is conditioned to this short-term, objective way of reasoning, it is possible to learn to develop right-brain, strategic thinking as well.

Characteristics of Right-Brain Thinking

In the right-brain outlook are many additional valuable characteristics. From our graphic on page 27, we can see that long-term, more subjective thinking comes from the right side of the brain. In the arena of Business Development, some very important abstract concepts require the contribution of right-brain thinking: those of mission, principles, Purpose and roles.

When a Business Development Professional has a propensity toward short-term thinking and planning, his capacity to recognize and act upon long-term opportunities is constrained.

Right-brain thinkers generally are intuitive and very creative. They are long-term, strategic, "why" thinkers. They are more interested in the abstract and philosophical aspects of a given situation, while the left-brain thinker is more interested in the nuts and bolts of the same situation. The right-brain thinker will generally see a situation from a position of abundance. For example, a right-brain thinker sees the universe of business prospects as infinite.

Further Balancing

As we now see, we all have the capacity in the brain for both long-term, subjective and short-term, objective thinking.   For success as a Business Development Professional, we must avail ourselves of the benefits of thinking from both sides of the brain. The left and right sides are compatible and must be used in tandem to provide the maximum benefit.

Principles

Mission

Purpose

Roles

**RIGHT HEMISPHERE
LONG-TERM SUBJECTIVE**

To be successful in Business Development, for example, you need to think left-brain in terms of Goals, plans, systems and skills. But even more importantly, you need to think right-brain in terms of principles, mission, Purpose and roles. By using this more balanced method of thinking, you are doubling your access to your inherent abilities.

For example, a predominantly left-brain-thinking person may be in a situation in which having a clear understanding and articulation of his Purpose – to help his clients meet their needs – could be used to maximum advantage. Being able to communicate this Purpose to a prospect could open up much broader opportunities. However, since this person thinks only in the short term, he has not considered this course of action. While he may subscribe to some vague notion about wanting to help his clients, he doesn't think of operating in light of this Purpose – and articulating this Purpose to his client – as being appropriate or helpful. He is preoccupied with his own short-term Goals and forgets what may be best in the long term for his client.

Conversely, an exclusively long-term thinker may have an excellent, broad-based relationship with a client, but fail to capitalize on a short-term opportunity for lack of specific skills. Being a right-brain thinker only, this individual may not focus enough on systems and skills and, consequently, may not quite be up to the challenge of everyday opportunities. She may understand the big picture, but have only a sketchy idea of how to capitalize on it in the short term.

Top-level performers in Professional Business Development - the top 3 percent that we call Professional Business Partners - have learned both left-brain, quantitative and right- brain, qualitative perspectives. They have learned to define what principles they stand for. They have developed their own personal mission statement, mastered goal-setting and planning, and learned to understand their Purpose in Business Development in balance with their Goals. They view Business Development from a perspective of abundance and from a position that seeks a mutually beneficial relationship for all partners. These are the characteristics that make a Professional Business Partner extremely valuable to his or her employer.

For success as a Business Development Professional, we must avail ourselves of the benefits of thinking from both sides of the brain.

These characteristics are fundamentally important for Professional Business Development people to be successful. Let's look at them from another perspective.

In his book, *Seven Habits of Highly Effective People*, Stephen Covey says that one of these habits is "beginning with the end in mind." He provides this vivid example: Visualize yourself as having died. During your wake, if someone were to read your eulogy, if someone was to speak of you as you have performed and lived and exemplified certain principles in your life, what would they say you would have stood for?

This process of thinking at the end and working back is valuable for people who want to develop to a high level of Professional Business Development. By reflecting from this perspective, they define certain principles that they chose to live their lives by – in all their roles, including the role of Business Development. From this they can develop a personal mission statement, a personal constitution of the tenets by which they want to behave in all their roles. By having this benchmark, they are able to measure the quality of their performance on a daily basis. And by defining these basic core principles and a personal mission statement, they create a benchmark against which they can measure the mission of any company they work for.

As an effective Business Development Professional, you must be anchored in your own defining principles. You must have a benchmark against which you measure your mission and that of the organization you choose to become involved with. You must be able to tell whether or not your principles and theirs are congruent. If they are, you make the free choice to be in the role of Business Development with the organization of your choosing. If not, it is inevitable that you will go your separate ways.

Top-level performers in Professional Business Development - the top 3 percent that we call Professiona Business Partners have learned both left-brain, quantitative and right-brain, qualitative perspectives.

What are the basic principles that define who you are? This is a strictly personal question. Assuming the basic tenets of human decency, there are no absolute answers. Your defining principles depend solely on who you are – as a person and as an executive charged with the mission of Business Development. Some considerations are:

- Honesty
- Sincerity
- Integrity
- Standing by your word
- Being true to yourself
- Doing what you do well and enjoying it
- Approaching life with a win-win perspective

These are only a few possible considerations. Ask yourself for others. What are the basic principles for which you hold yourself accountable in every area of your life? In the final analysis, what do you stand for? Business Development Goals not based on your own personal principles will have little, if any, meaning for you, and you will soon find yourself in conflict.

As an effective Business Development Professional, you must be anchored in your own defining principles.

Setting Goals: Your Road Map

Once you are clear in your own mind about your principles and mission, and their congruency with the principles of your organization, you're in a position to set Goals for your role in Business Development. Goals are your road map. Whether you define them as income per quarter, calls per week, or yearly salary increases, they help you define and reach your personal career objectives. Without these there is no provision to gauge success or recognize when you have achieved it. However, surprisingly, very few people have clearly defined Goals – either for their role in Business Development or for the rest of their lives.

To be meaningful, your Goals must have three characteristics: They must be conceivable, believable and achievable. Remember this: If your mind can conceive it and you can believe it, then you can achieve it.

What is your goal in Business Development? Here is an interesting exercise designed as a basic focus for goal-setting. We will cover this in greater detail in Chapter 4. However, it can be quite helpful to learn now and keep as a reminder throughout your career in Professional Business Development. It's called the Life Line Exercise.

Take a piece of paper and draw a horizontal line from left to right. At the left end, mark Point A and enter here the year you were born. At the opposite end, mark Point D to represent the year you expect to die. Pick out a point where you are now on the life line, based on the amount of years you expect to live. That's Point B. The time from Point A to Point B is over, but it has provided you an abundance of experiences. You have the wisdom of those years as well as any conceptual limitations carried through those years that may still hinder you in all your roles.

Point B is ever-moving. Every day you move closer to Point D. Somewhere between B and D, pick Point C. That's the year you intend to retire, having attained financial independence. This doesn't mean you will never work again in your life. It simply means you will not have to work.

Here's your challenge: What vehicle or role in life will you choose to take you from B, where you are now, to C, where you are financially independent? Of course, the role of Professional Business Development is an excellent role to help you achieve this goal. However, you must decide for yourself if Professional Business Development is the right role for you.

Goals are your road map. They help you define and reach your personal career objectives.

By using both sides of your brain and planning short-term objectives and actions that will help you reach your long-term Goals, you can keep a clear view of what you're doing and why you're doing it throughout your Business Development career. The distinction between your Goals and your Purpose in Business Development is an important one. Your Goals are short-term with specific plans for action, while your Purpose is a long-term concept that focuses your short-term plans and actions.

Just as the Life Line Exercise illustrates, success in your role of Professional Business Development will require that you make use of both short-term and long-term thinking. You need to develop short-term objectives that will help you accomplish your personal long-term goal of financial independence. And you'll need a long-term perspective to envision that goal and to take the long view when helping your customers reach their Goals.

To be meaningful, your Goals must have 3 characteristics: They must be conceivable, believable and achievable.

However, having Goals, even with the related plan and Business Development System, is not enough to ensure success. Victor Frankl wrote in *Man's Search for Meaning* that "No man can endure the how if he does not know the why." And that's true. The price of success is much too high to pay unless you know why you want to pay it. The "how" is short-term. The "why" is long-term. Learning how to be successful in Business Development is such a painful, long-term process that if you don't have a "why" to sustain you, you're not going to make it. No one ever succeeds at mastering the process of Business Development without knowing why he wants to master it.

THE LIFE LINE

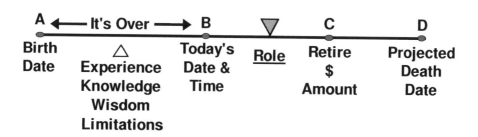

Finding the answer to the "why" question is determining your Purpose in Professional Business Development. Your Purpose is quite different from your Goals. Goals are short-term, self-serving, internally focused, based on "what's in it for me." Goals that are based on making the sale whatever the cost will soon expose themselves as being superficial. They are reactionary and generally motivated by external forces. They are based on the moment at hand—a series of one-shot deals with little or no regard for the future. Professional Business Development must be based on your long-term Purpose of helping your customer solve his or her problems. Your fundamental Purpose as a professional in Business Development is to help the prospect or client discover what he or she needs or wants – regardless of whether or not you have it – and to help him or her find a way to get it. Your Purpose in Business Development is what's in it for someone else. If you help a client meet his or her needs, he or she will help you meet your own financial and career Goals. It's as simple as that.

Consider this example: A large manufacturing plant wants to upgrade some of its processing equipment. A salesperson with only short-term Goals, whose company has only one type of equipment, becomes aware of this opportunity and appears at the plant to present his line. He tours the plant with the manager and goes through the motions of assessing needs.

Success in your role of Professional Business Development will require that you make use of both short-term and long-term thinking.

Based on this quick impression, he immediately recommends his line of processing equipment, which is available only through him. In extolling the merits of this line, he finds himself compromising with the truth. This is his idea of a stretch. He convinces himself he's not really lying. He quotes a price and makes the sale.

His price turns out to be low because the equipment is not ideally suited for the complete needs of the client. It will do part of the job adequately, but in order to do what the plant needs to do, additional engineering will be required and additional equipment must be installed to handle another phase of the processing. The additional engineering and equipment will allow his line of equipment to do a mediocre job on its particular phase, but it is slow and not geared for the heavy demands of the plant. The additional engineering work and investment in upgrade equipment is time consuming. His line is simply not suited to this application. After a while, the plant must replace it or live with a reduction in production – not a pleasant choice.

"No man can endure the how if he does not know the why." – Victor Frankl

Meanwhile, a Professional Business Partner encounters this prospect and begins probing for problems and pain. He communicates early in his relationship his Purpose for contacting the client: to help him figure out what he needs or wants and help him find a way to get it – regardless of whom he purchases it from. The Professional Business Partner also communicates his goal of developing a mutually beneficial business relationship, if appropriate. He is operating with, and communicates, a fundamental balance of Purpose and Goals. Executing the Professional Business Development System, which includes extensive discussions with the engineering manager, the Professional Business Partner is soon aware of the problems the company is facing.

After personally inspecting the plant and becoming familiar with the operation, the Professional Business Partner is able to make a proposal within a few days. His proposal involves replacing an older piece of processing equipment with the recently purchased one that is ill-suited in its present utilization, but would be sufficient in place of the older machine. The purchase of new equipment that is designed for the work the inferior machine was doing then is necessary. For this manufacturing company, it means purchasing another piece of equipment a year or so earlier than had been anticipated, but the benefits of increased production will go a long way toward defraying the cost. The recently purchased equipment sold by the earlier salesperson can be used to upgrade total production. All in all, everyone involved is reasonably benefitted, even the salesperson who took the order without really addressing the long-term needs of the customer. But who will be first considered when additional equipment is required? The Professional Business Partner or the salesperson?

Professional Business Development must be based on your long-term Purpose of helping your customer solve his or her problems.

Salespeople who reach some short-term monetary Goals by being very self-centered and internally focused frequently get the sale at any cost. But these individuals don't last long, and they seldom have repeat customers. They're always hustling for the next sale, and they're not likely to get referrals. They typically operate with a philosophy of scarcity, believing, "There's only so much business, so I'd better get my share immediately. This might be my last opportunity."

Professional Business Development must be based on your long-term Purpose of helping your customer solve his or her problems.

Business Development Professionals who understand their Purpose in balance with their Goals, however, think differently. They focus on different ends. They are client-focused rather than self-focused. They have a personal mission statement to guide their behavior that helps them balance the long-term needs of the client with their short-term Goals in Business Development. They have learned to think like business people, not salespeople.

They have business relationships with clients on a win-win basis, and they are treated like Professional business people. They are working to help the client or prospect be successful. They operate from a mental perspective of abundance. They have learned that when they help clients meet their needs, the clients will help them reach their financial Goals.

These Business Development Professionals have come to understand a basic truth:

MBD *insights*

You must always put your Purpose ahead of your Goals.

4

Identity-Role Differentiation

One of the most critical factors for success in Professional Business Development is the ability to separate ourselves from our roles – to distinguish between who we are and what we do. Understanding and managing role confusion is one of the most important tasks you face as a professional committed to Business Development.

For example, during your lifetime you may have filled many roles – spouse, parent, relative, friend, neighbor, owner, manager, executive, etc. How do you separate these role-identities from your self-identity? It's not an easy task. And much of our early learning may make it more difficult. The following exercise shows you just how difficult separating role from self can be:

Suppose you win a trip to a Caribbean island. You're walking a sandy beach, looking out over crystal clear water under blue skies. It's 87 degrees, and you're sitting under a palm tree running your fingers through the sand. Nothing to threaten you for miles. Just pure enjoyment.

But there's a hitch. To win the trip, you had to leave behind all your roles. You had to give up the role of husband or wife, parent, sister, brother, friend, neighbor, engineer, owner, chef, manager. You're on this island alone, with out any of your roles. On a scale of 0 to 10, what number would you choose to represent the value you place on the part of you that's on the island – alone, without any roles?

Most people in our workshops feel defined by their roles and judged by others accordingly. Most have never been forced to recognize the difference between role-identity and self-identity. They have labored under the premise that who they are and what they do are intertwined and inseparable. This is usually a result of perceptions acquired early in life. Consequently, most answer about 3 on our 0 to 10 scale, ranking their self-identity as fairly insignificant.

One of the most critical factors for success in Professional Business Development is the ability to separate ourselves from our roles – to distinguish between who we are and what we do. Understanding and managing role confusion is one of the most important tasks you face as a professional committed to Business Development.

Occasionally, someone will answer with what is a healthier approach to this puzzle. That's the person who feels his or her value without any roles is at the higher end of the scale – maybe even 10. This person is saying, "I like myself regardless of what my roles are. My roles don't make me anything. Roles aren't that important."

Roles begin when we're very young. Parents and teachers reward us for what we do. Johnny doesn't spill his oatmeal. Sarah gets good grades. Bobby makes the basketball team. "We're proud of you," say the adults. And as children, most of us begin to believe that how we do in our roles is how we are defined as an individual. Our role-identity and our self-identity become meshed together and we begin to think of them as one. Half the people who go through the Caribbean island exercise in our workshops, for example, cannot even picture themselves on the island without any roles.

The relatively few who answer near or at the top of the scale have defined themselves and their value independently of their roles. They have accepted and like themselves just as much in or out of their roles, and they are aware of the difference between role-identity and self-identity.

All people come into this world as "10s," with no negatives to lower their self-worth. But as their lives progress, many begin to see themselves as less than 10s as their role performance comes under attack from critical parents and others. Success – especially for the Business Development executive – demands a self-perception relatively near 10 regardless of any consideration of roles.

Success – especially for the Business Development executive – demands a self-perception relatively near 10 regardless of any consideration of roles.

The Psychological Winner

Those in our island exercise who score their self-identity as being between 7 and 10 are what we might call psychological winners and are generally successful in their individual roles. For the most part, they have made good choices in their roles. They have sorted out most of the emotional baggage they possess, and they like themselves and are satisfied with their performance in their roles. Consequently, with training, they can become very successful. They rise to the top as CEOs, corporate officers and executives, civic and political leaders. Their success in one role propagates success in other roles for them.

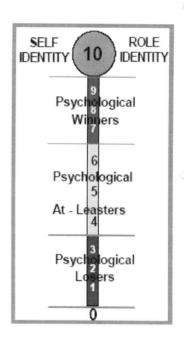

Donna Duwell, a corporate executive representing an upscale manufacturer of ladies clothing, is one of these. As a little girl, Donna had an unusual interest in fashion magazines, modeling, and high-quality, stylish clothing. She knew at an early age that was where her professional interests were. Her role choice was easy and a good one for her. Like most of us, she had some emotional baggage, albeit a relatively small amount. However, she has explored that emotional baggage and how she acquired it, and has been able to separate that baggage from her various roles. It has little, if any, effect on her role as a Business Development Professional.

Further, she enjoys the challenge and contacts of her profession and the opportunity to solve clients' problems. She also is proud of the product and service she represents. She happens to have a degree in her field, as well as other professional training. She is primarily centered on marketing, but also has input in design and most other important areas of her company's operations. She is the epitome of success in her professional capacity and an asset to her corporation and industry.

This success carries over into other roles for her – mother, wife, charity fundraiser, friend, caretaker and others, which she performs as necessary. The transfer of success from role to role allows Donna to consider herself a near 10 on the self-worth scale.

MBD *insights*

Success breeds success.

The Psychological Loser

Those who see themselves as psychological losers have done poorly in their roles and will usually score themselves 0 to 3 on our performance scale.

Though there are many influences comprising the losers' roles, much of the responsibility rests with poor choices and the inability to differentiate self from individual roles. Consequently, there is a negative build-up that flows from role to role. As psychological losers struggle with few positive results, they begin to see themselves as poor performers in most of their roles.

Stanley Shortfall is one of these. He is a building materials salesman for a less than triple-A firm. Stanley accepted his current position because it offers a few more dollars per week than his previous situation. There is little opportunity to move up with this company, and the industry is not one he enjoys or in which he even has much more than a passing interest. The job is a poor choice on Stanley's part. As a result, he rarely makes a sale.

This predicament leads to very few positive tangible results and is devastating to what is left of Stanley's self-confidence. This perception of failure also carries over into his other roles in life.

Stanley soon finds himself in a not-so-hot marriage, and he has begun to drink too much. He is unable to separate any of the roles he has chosen for himself – or, more accurately, stumbled into – and sees himself as a loser in all of them. He has some real problems, mostly caused by poor choices and the role confusion that he doesn't understand. He is hurting, but he doesn't know why.

The Psychological At-Leaster

Psychological At-Leasters score themselves between 3 and 7 on the self-evaluation scale. They are not winners, but to them, not losing is a victory of sorts. They go through the motions and play their role, but never at the risk of taking a risk. They are more than willing to capitulate, or at least acquiesce, in challenging situations.

Melvin Mediocre is a representative for a wholesale grocer. He is following in the footsteps of his father, Motley Mediocre, who had the same job as Melvin until his retirement from the firm after 25 years. Melvin feels safe here, just as his father did.

Melvin makes most of his calls at individual stores instead of the corporate headquarters of the of the grocery chains. This is more comfortable for him, as he feels less threatened by a possible rejection. At each store, the manager – if he's not busy – might offer coffee and an exchange of pleasantries, and Melvin can take the order, which is already prepared for him to pick up. If the manager isn't available to Melvin, he can talk with someone on a lower echelon. This way he can still take the order and receive the same degree of satisfaction without the risk involved in calling on the corporate higher-ups and chancing some feeling of rejection that terrifies him.

Melvin is a chip off the old block, and this is the chief reason for his choice of this professional role. He is in a situation that demands little, but he will be an early casualty should economic constraints negatively affect his company. He is dispensable and, at this point, ill-equipped for other professional roles. Melvin is vulnerable. He feels safe in his 3 to 7 arena of performance. Emotional baggage? He hasn't a clue. Even if he did, it would be much too frightening for him to explore. Melvin might wonder a little about life beyond his 7, but he won't risk an effort to find it. He wants to stay above the 3 – at all costs – in all his roles. He won't run from real success, but it will have to find him first if he experiences it. After all, it's too risky the other way for the Psychological At-Leaster.

MBD *insights*

"Ofttimes nothing profits more than self-esteem, grounded on just and right, well managed." – John Milton

Why Self-Identity Matters

Why is this matter of role-identity and self-identity important in Business Development? Because a person who confuses role-identity with self-identity will find it difficult to put himself or herself in the high-risk situations that successful Business Development requires. He or she may avoid contact with potential prospects for fear of failure – role-failure that, because the individual confuses it with self-failure, will threaten his or her self-concept.

To break out of one's "comfort zone," to risk calling the president instead of the janitor, requires separating role-failure from self-worth. If you can separate the two and develop a healthy self-concept, you will be successful in whatever role you choose.

A person who confuses role-identity with self-identity will find it difficult to put himself or herself in the high-risk situations that successful Business Development requires.

Successful achievement in Professional Business Development dictates the separation of role-identity and self-identity. Your performance in the role of a Business Development Professional should be isolated from your other roles and your self-identity as much as possible. You are performing a unique role that should stand alone without the confusion of your other identities. Your role as a spouse or a family member, for example, is independent of your role as a professional executive or any of your other roles.

An "At-Leaster" level of 3 to 7 on the self-concept scale will pretty much preclude any risk-taking. If this concept is allowed to take hold and influence your professional role, it will be very difficult for you to do the essential risk-taking that is demanded from the successful Business Development Professional. For the At-Leaster, there is a good chance any rejection, for whatever reason, will be taken personally.

This role confusion, coupled with a low self-concept, can lead to failure in Business Development because an individual can perform in his or her roles only in a manner that is consistent with that individual's self-concept. Say an individual operates at the "At-Leaster" level of around 5. Sometimes she feels good about herself and sometimes she doesn't. You train her in some dynamite Business Development skills. She goes out and makes six sales calls resulting in six sales. In her Business Development role, she is now functioning as a 10. But her self-concept is still a 5. What will she do? Since she made six sales, she'll have to find a way to miss six sales. Her self-concept will not allow her to remain a 10 for very long. She must always operate within her comfort zone, and that zone, as yet, does not reach up to 10. To be successful in Professional Business Development, you must realize there is a major difference in who you "I" – your identity – and who you "R"– your role. You must develop a self-concept that sees identity as a constant 10, thus allowing Business Development role performance at that level.

An individual can perform in his or her roles only in a manner that is consistent with that individual's self-concept.

To be successful in Professional Business Development, you must realize there is a major difference in who you "I" – your identity – and who you "R" – your role.

A client without pain or a problem or the perception thereof has legitimate grounds for rejection of a proposal. This is based on the client's awareness and on good business practices and in no way should be construed as a personal rejection for the Business Development Professional. However, a person with an At-Leaster 3 to 7 self-worth score coupled with role confusion will likely view the rejection as a personal failure and will be reluctant to take future chances that extend beyond the safe, comfortable area.

Those who can develop a self-perception at the 10 level and separate their self-identity and professional roles have the basic psychological formula for success. A 10 will not operate on a 5 level very long without moving back into the more challenging area of the 10. A self-defined 5 who has, for whatever reason, experienced brief success at the 10 level, will make an unconscious effort to migrate back to the safe area or comfort zone.

Secrets of Role Success – And Failure
Why do people succeed or fail in their chosen roles? Why will you find it easy or difficult to succeed in Professional Business Development – or any of the other roles you may play in your life? The reasons are simple, but not easily managed. They are often rooted in early childhood, and they require constant examination of your attitudes and actions to be sure you are working toward maximum success.

Reasons for Success
First, individuals must make a free and informed choice of their roles. This is essential for success in any role, including that of the Business Development Professional. There also must be in place a discernible and unmistakable awareness of the difference between self-identity and role-identity. The Professional Business Development role provides no vehicle for meeting emotional or personal needs or enhancing feelings of self-worth. It is completely separate from these considerations.

Those who can develop a self-perception at the 10 level and separate their self-identity and professional roles have the basic psychological formula for success.

The separation of the roles must include, at all times, the individual's awareness of which role he or she is performing. Confusion among the roles will create an unnecessary added burden that hinders success. One can only perform in one role at a time. The Business Development Professional's role may incorporate the roles of manager, advisor, administrator, service person and many others. Success requires functioning in these individual roles at various times. If, for example, you are required to complete a performance evaluation for your Business Development team members, you must stress that your critique is offered and should be accepted from a professional point of view and relates only to the team member's role performance. It is no reflection of anyone's self-worth.

Reasons for Failure

Generally, people fail in their roles for one or a combination of three major reasons. First, some make poor choices of their roles in life. They fall in love very young and get married. Their infatuation holds for a while. They are lucky if their marriage survives beyond this point. They choose a career role without truly knowing their own strengths and weaknesses, even their own preferences. It is not unusual to find a struggling accountant, for example, who has entered the field because his father had been an accountant, not realizing that his talents and natural affinities make him far better suited to be a commercial artist. He would make a great artist, but will probably be a mediocre accountant at best. Since many of us make career choices before we know ourselves fully, it may take us several years to figure out why it's so difficult to succeed in our roles. Many times, we have simply made a poor or uninformed choice, influenced by family or friends or the chance opportunities that have presented themselves to us.

Individuals must make a free and informed choice of their roles.

One can only perform in one role at a time.

One of the major reasons for failure in Professional Business Development is an initial poor choice of an individual's professional role. This can be true of failure in many roles of life – i.e., marriage, friends, habits, investments -almost any important facet of life.

As we saw from our examples of Stanley and Melvin, both stumbled into their professional situations with little forethought or reason for their choices of roles. Little consideration was given to how well-suited, really interested, or even capable each was in the choice of his respective role. Uninformed choices were made that alone may consign them to function as Losers or At-Leasters.

Another major reason for role failure is that we receive poor training in our roles. For example, when did you learn to be a parent? Primarily from infancy to six years of age. In spite of all the books and articles you've read since then, how often do you hear yourself telling your kids what you heard from your parents? Poor role training will lead you down the path of failure. Many people enter their roles in life with little or no preparation or training other than what they've gleaned from their parents, and this mostly in the early, pre-school, formative years. This often shows up later as negative emotional baggage.

Similarly, we oftentimes receive poor training in our career roles. Successful business people are often dispatched with great urgency to go out and do Business Development without the slightest instruction in how to do it. Apparently their managers think that success as an engineer or division manager or technical manager ensures success as a Business Development Professional. But, while this course cautions against reliance on a superficial, gimmicky system of sales techniques, some training in the fundamentals of Business Development is essential. We are not simply born knowing how to develop business. Poor training in any role is a reliable predictor of failure. If we weren't born with it, didn't get it at home or from formal education or experience, then chances are we didn't get it. Some degree of training in the fundamentals of Business Development is vital to success in the many roles of the Professional Business Development executive.

Substantial emotional baggage, if brought into the role, can be the most devastating factor leading to role failure. Even with a free and informed choice and adequate training, these emotional problems can still wreak havoc. The unchecked and unresolved attitudes, feelings, values and beliefs that usually come from early experiences in the formative years are intense and powerful. If allowed to creep into a professional role through the confusion of self-identity and professional identity, they cannot always be offset by good choices and good training. Emotional carryover must be recognized, dealt with, resolved and excluded from the professional role. Success in Business Development, and in life, bears a direct correlation to the ability to deal positively with this issue.

> *You simply learn more from your mistakes, if you can recognize them, than you will ever learn from your successes.*

Risking, Failing and Learning

Although, like most people, you probably fear failure in your professional role, you really should welcome it. You don't learn as much as quickly from succeeding as you learn from failing. You simply learn more from your mistakes, if you can recognize them, than you will ever learn from your successes. You have to risk failure in order to succeed.

Risking

Webster defines "risk" as "exposure to danger or hazard" or "the possibility of loss or injury."

In Professional Business Development, we define risking as loosening your hold on the certain to strive for something that is better, even if it's uncertain that you will attain it.

Not risking is the surest way of losing. Never play not to lose; always play to win. A life without risk, always comfortable, is a life without growth. Remember Melvin? He played it close to the vest, to use a poker term, never risking and subsequently never experiencing growth. He played to stay above the 3 level on the self-worth chart, never risking anything that might lift him above 7. There is no growth without risk.

Many of us avoid risking because there is at least a little psychological discomfort associated with it. The danger of failure is frightening, but the challenge of reward can be exhilarating. Some people actually enjoy the stimulation of walking on the edge, of laying their skills on the line in a high-stakes situation and winning success. People who enjoy this intrigue are near-10s on the identity chart.

In Professional Business Development, we define risking as loosening your hold on the certain to strive for something that is better, even if it's uncertain that you will attain it.

Their confidence serves them well. In addition to successful performance as Business Development executives, they also enjoy psychological growth.

If you are not in the career you desire, it is time to risk. If you are not happy in a life situation that you are in, you have to do something to make it better. When the pain of change is less than the pain you are in, you will change.

Remember, however, that there is a difference between risk and sacrifice. You sacrifice when you give a greater value for a lesser one. Never sacrifice, and never take a risk that is bigger than you can afford to lose. The key to intelligent risking is accurate assessment of your risk versus your reward. If you risk psychological discomfort to gain financial and professional success, that's clearly a risk worth taking. Don't let yourself plod along at a 5 performance level when in your heart you know you can be a 10.

MBD *insights*

⚜*You have to risk failure in order to achieve success.*

Failing

The real successes are often people who have learned the lessons of failure, for failure has much to teach the astute learner. For one thing, the reasons for the failure are usually painfully obvious. Thus the conscientious individual can readily learn how to avoid that particular failure again. But perhaps the most important lesson is that the individual can fail and still survive to try again. Typically there are five steps associated with encountering failure:

When the pain of change is less than the pain you are in, you will change.

- Disbelief – No one strives to fail or plans to fail. When it happens, the immediate reaction is, "I can't believe this!" Failing is a shock because there was little anticipation of failure, and rightfully so. Because most people don't anticipate or consider the possibility of failure, the immediate reaction is not to accept the reality. However, reality does not go away.

- Fear – Fear forces us to examine the consequences of this failure and the negative potential it could have on our future. We think, "There goes my career." Fear causes us to anticipate the worst. We overestimate the outcome of the failure. Because we are not prepared to deal with it, all of our emotional baggage and insecurities rise to the surface and begin to cloud our thinking. But fear has value in that it is a short-term motivator that brings about action.

- Anger – Quite often following fear, which is the first component of the "fight-or-flight" reaction, comes anger. Anger is usually manifested externally. There may be a tendency to blame others or the situation for the condition you are in. This is a natural feeling, as the failure is not fully understood at this point. The choice between blaming or acting is critical. The individual who externalizes the cause of his situation will tend to blame others and become paralyzed, while the individual who begins to internalize the situation will become angry at it, begin to accept it and move toward a solution.

- Acceptance and Analysis – At this point the individual will say, "Well, it has happened, and it isn't going to get any better without my taking responsibility for it and bringing about a different outcome." This is the rational realization that failure has occurred. The individual realizes that there is little hope of reversing the failure and that it would be best to move on into exploring the reasons for it, as well as possible positive outcomes. This is the healthiest attitude at this point.

The individual is now in a position to try to understand and learn from the failure. The situation can be turned into a valuable learning tool. At this point, the Business Development Professional recognizes failure as an opportunity. If she has lost a significant, anticipated contract, for example, this is the opportunity to reexamine her script and take inventory of working tools and other assets and their utilization. This analysis may be revealing. It offers a chance for an illuminating review.

Managing for Success in Business Development

If during your career you are called on to manage a team of Business Development Professionals, you can boost your team's chances for success by thoughtfully applying the lessons we've talked about in this chapter. Helping people separate self-identity from role-identity is critical in developing a Business Development team. Individuals in Business Development cannot succeed in that role if they are trying to validate their self-worth or get their emotional needs met. As you become part of the creation and development of a successful Business Development team, keep the following identity role-management rules in mind:

■ *Each individual must make a free and informed choice of his or her role.* Too many people are in Business Development because they failed at something else and were put there as a last resort. They have backed into the role. That's the wrong decision made by the wrong person. Reject this situation if you can.

■ *Each individual on the team must have goals and plans for his or her Business Development role.* Goals and plans help people accept individual responsibility and keep the Business Development role separate from the other roles in their lives. But your team members cannot accept responsibility unless they have a healthy self-concept. Managers must never question a person's self-worth. They have no right to. Always reinforce the person's "I" side – his or her identity. Help your team members establish, develop and reinforce a healthy self-concept, and they will do infinitely better in whatever role they ultimately determine is in their best interest. A person who sees his or her self-worth as a 10 won't have any failures – only temporary setbacks. Such a person won't fail because he or she won't quit.

■ *Each individual on the team must know what role he or she is in at all times.* A confused Business Development person sells nothing. A buyer who deals with a confused Business Development person buys nothing. A confused Business Development manager trying to manage a confused Business Development person is simply trying to manage confusion. This is a proven formula for disaster.

■ *Each individual can only function and be managed in one role at a time.* Role separation is critical for several reasons. If people fail in their Business Development role, it must not reflect on their self-worth. They cannot look at their role this way unless they are able to separate their Business Development role from their self-identity. As a manager required to criticize an employee's performance on the team, make sure your team member understands that the critical evaluation has nothing to do with him as a person. While functioning in your Business Development manager role, you are dealing with him in his Business Development role. When people equate their role to their self-worth, their shields will go up and their emotions will get in the way of learning.

■ *Each individual on the team must have the right to fail and learn.* Only someone with a solid self-concept will risk failure. As we have continually emphasized, failure is a necessary ingredient of success. You must first learn to fail. Otherwise, you will fail to learn. You must begin to understand that it's OK to fail. Build a self-concept healthy enough to risk failure. Otherwise, you will never succeed. Thomas Edison once stated, "I have had a lot of success with failure." In perfecting the light bulb, Edison experienced 10,000 failures before he finally succeeded. A friend remarked that 10,000 failures made an astounding total. Edison replied, "I successfully eliminated, 10,000 times, materials and combinations that wouldn't work." That could only happen with an individual who clearly understands the importance of separating role-identity from self-worth.

> *You must first learn to fail.*
> *Other-wise, you will fail to learn.*

■ *Never question the individual's self-worth.* Always reinforce it. Help your other team members establish, develop and maintain a healthy self-concept. They will do measurably better in whatever role they determine is best for them. Their success in Professional Business Development is impossible without a healthy self-concept.

■ *Each individual must work on the right end of the problem.* Most people seek a simple mechanical solution to any problem. They think the right techniques or skills will lead to success. Help your team members learn this valuable lesson: Whenever there is lack of success, WE are the problem. The problem is not the economy or the customer or the product. It's always us. Don't waste time working on the wrong end of the problem. Work on the right end – the conceptual end. Begin exploring and improving the limiting attitudes, feelings, values and beliefs you carry as emotional limitations. Work on your "I" side, learn to discover and appreciate your identity apart from your roles, and your "R" side will inevitably benefit. Work as hard as you can on your business role and even harder on yourself. Personal growth is the root of growth in any career. It is essential for enjoying success in Professional Business Development.

Work as hard as you can on your business role and even harder on yourself.

■ *You can only help those who want to help themselves.* If your team members are looking for someone to help them more than they are willing to help themselves, they have a problem. Each of us must take ownership and responsibility for our own problems. Doing something about them is the individual's own choice, and they are accountable for the results of their problem solving.

5

Goal-Setting and Motivation

Setting meaningful goals can make your entire life, both personal and professional, more satisfying and more successful. In Professional Business Development, Goal-Setting is not just a desirable option. Successful Business Development demands setting significant goals and investing the effort to attain them.

Successful Business Development demands setting significant goals and investing the effort to attain them.

When you actively work to set and accomplish clearly visualized goals, you simply achieve more. You arise each morning with a clear vision of what you want to get done that day, and you know why you want to get those things done. You always have an end result in mind. Accomplishment takes less time and energy when you are focused on carrying out specific actions to achieve specific goals.

Goals, while a professional necessity, can also enhance your personal life when personally set and sought. When you learn to incorporate your personal and professional goals into a concerted, overall, purposeful effort, you truly begin to live an intentional and successful life.

The pursuit of meaningful and well-defined goals is rewarded by a higher achievement quotient than would otherwise be attainable. This discipline gives you the benefit of knowing why, when, where and how you will proactively approach your daily endeavors.

Other personal benefits can include, but are not limited to, higher income, improved health, better relationships, and general contentment and satisfaction. It is difficult to overstate the degree to which these benefits accrue as a result of pursuing meaningful and realistic goals.

Goal-Setting is an absolute requirement for success as a Professional in Business Development. In the context of Goal-Setting, failure for Business Development people can come in two forms. It can result from failing to achieve your goals or from failing to know what your goals are. A blueprint for failure by the Business Development Professional consists of the lack of recognizable goals and/or the inability to bring such goals to fulfillment. Any time you fail to achieve a Business Development goal, you should carefully examine the situation and determine why. If the reason for failure can be determined, it likely can be corrected and a valuable lesson can be learned. The more fundamental failure even to identify and set goals is an oversight that leads almost inevitably down the path of business failure.

MBD *insights*

An indefinable goal cannot be achieved.

Not only does the set-and-achieve process give you the opportunity to evaluate your success, it also enables you to avoid a distraction that could be misconstrued as an opportunity. With clearly defined goals, you can determine very early on if a situation meets the criteria of your goals and is worth pursuing. If it is compatible with your goals and possesses potential, you will be motivated to persevere. However, if there is no congruence, you will quickly recognize that your time could be spent more effectively. Thus your goals can serve as a means of qualifying situations, opportunities and even individuals.

Yogi Berra, a member of the Baseball Hall of Fame, observed, "If you don't know where you're going, you may end up someplace else." Setting and pursuing realistic and meaningful goals can save you from this fate. If you have Goals and Plans for achieving them, making decisions is easy. You have a built-in gauge to measure every opportunity. If it has potential to advance you toward your goals, you move toward it wholeheartedly. If it doesn't fit with your goals, you pass it up without a second thought.

Without goals you may not even recognize an opportunity that offers great potential for you. If you view the world through unfocused eyes, your vision may not be sharp enough to see the possibilities. But with clearly set and energetically pursued goals, you will be amazed at how often you run into what seems like a simple stroke of good luck. Another famous athletic figure, Pennsylvania State University's successful head football coach Joe Paterno, tells his players, "Luck is preparation meeting opportunity." Taking this a step further, we offer:

MBD *insights*

To a great extent, we create our own luck.

What seems like good luck is simply an opportunity viewed through the motivated eye of the professional with a clear view of the goal.

Setting a Flight Plan for Success

An aircraft without a flight plan, without a pilot who follows the plan, and without instruments to monitor progress, can be driven by the wind to an unpredictable destination. Your career as a Professional in Business Development is much the same. Without a plan, your professional life can wander aimlessly, driven this way and that by chance alone.

But a flight plan only has value when the pilot who uses it accepts personal ownership of it and feels a sense of responsibility for carrying it out. Many people who find themselves thrust into a career in Business Development have not accepted responsibility for their own success. Consider the different levels of responsibility implied in the following statements:

- I wish my life were better.

- I want my life to be better.

- I will make my life better.

It is amazing how many people, who state with great conviction that they entered the field of Business Development so they could be their own bosses, have yet to take the first step toward accepting personal responsibility for their success. They blame their failures on the product, the market, the customer, or other factors, denying themselves the rewards of a job well done. Successful Business Development people, on the other hand, know that they alone are responsible for their success or failure. They have learned the truth of the often-quoted maxim, "If it is to be, it's up to me."

Like the skilled pilot, you must follow your own flight plan for success. And, just as the pilot checks the map for obstacles – mountains, towers and the like – you must consider what factors will be obstacles to your success. Your competitors' strengths, your territory size, seasonal variances, government regulations, limitations of your product or your own lack of knowledge may slow down your progress toward your goal. But for the shortest road to success, look first for your internal limitations that will hinder your progress.

For example, do you have a knowledge of the Four Cornerstones for success in Business Development? Do you have sufficient technical, business, people and money knowledge? Do you understand the principal differences between the concepts of "role" and "self"? Have you mastered the other eight competencies required for being a Professional in Business Development? As we discussed in Chapter 2, these are: Principles, Mission, Purpose, Roles, Goals, Plans, Systems and Skills. Once you have fully internalized these requirements for your success, then you may begin to look outside yourself for external factors that limit your progress.

But these obstacles –internal or external – do not preclude your success. Just like the knowledgeable pilot, you simply plan a way around or over them. Before you encounter these obstacles in the performance of your daily Business Development responsibilities, visualize yourself overcoming them. Think of exactly what actions you will take to minimize their effect and maximize your strengths. Then when you do meet them you will be prepared. Winning will be a simple matter of carrying out your plan and understanding the measure of your progress.

As you create your flight plan, consider, too, the best use of resources that are your fuel for flight. Professionals realize they don't operate in a vacuum, so they learn to draw on all the resources available to them: industry knowledge, customer knowledge, product knowledge, and application knowledge, as well as their Business Development System for interviewing and qualifying. They also realize the value of their support systems – Business Development support, client service, product analysis, contract administration and technical support people. And they make full use of top management – the Business Development managers, executives, marketing specialists and financial managers who can be useful reservoirs of information and expertise. Fueled by all of these resources, the Professional Business Development specialist rises above what others perceive to be insurmountable obstacles.

Charting Your Life Line

A prerequisite for setting meaningful goals is to understand where you are in your life right now. The simple exercise of the Life Line that we introduced to you briefly in Chapter 3 will help you evaluate your present life position and get a handle on where you want to go in the future and how you want to get there. Let's look at the Life Line Exercise in more detail:

Across the top of a page, draw a horizontal line. At the far left end, place an A and write down the year you were born. At the far right end, place a D and estimate the year you will probably die. If you have trouble thinking about this, you can play the odds and estimate the median life expectancy in the U.S. For men, it's about 76, and for women, about 78. On the continuum from left to right, move the appropriate distance that indicates your present age. Mark that spot with a B.

THE LIFE LINE

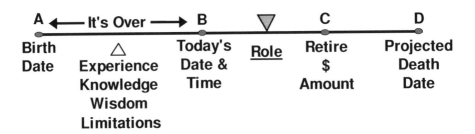

Now consider this: the time represented between Point A and B in your life is over. It is part of your history. For many of us it makes up a major part of who we are today. You will never have a chance to relive it, only to learn from it. Your ability to take your experiences, gain knowledge from them and apply them is the wisdom you bring to where you are today – Point B. The time represented between Points B and D is your future – what you have in your hand, the time you have left. Choose a year between Points B and D in which you will set the goal of financial independence so that you can financially retire. It doesn't mean you have to retire at that age – simply that you will have the option to retire financially. It is that time at which you will not have to work, if you so choose, and you have acquired sufficient personal net worth to achieve your goal of financial independence. Mark this as Point C, and write down the specific dollar amount that you believe it will take for you to achieve that level of financial independence. This will be the amount of net worth that will allow you to live off its interest – or principal plus interest – for the remainder of your life in the style you choose. Divide that figure by the number of years between Point B, today, and Point C. That's the amount of money you must acquire – beyond your annual expenses – each year in order to attain independence. Now you have a financial goal.

Your ability to take your experiences, gain knowledge from them and apply it is the wisdom you bring to where you are today.

Let's go a step further. Having decided on a financial goal and reflected on the number of years remaining to reach that goal, consider what professional role you could choose as your best vehicle for reaching your goal. What career will have the greatest likelihood of helping you reach your goal? Chances are you may choose a career as a Professional in Business Development, since that is where you find yourself today, and it is a career that offers significant earning potential. If you make a free and informed choice of a career in Professional Business Development, you will look at that career through new eyes. When you see your role as a vehicle for helping you attain your goals, you will know why you make those initial Business Development calls, why you must have a Business Development system, why you work on your emotional limitations and why you set Goals and Plans. You will have a clear idea of where you want to go in partnership with your company and how you intend to get there.

Placing your goals within a time frame serves in several ways. It puts your life into perspective from a time standpoint. We have all heard the old adage, "time is money." Thinking in terms of limitations on available time for achieving your financial goals presents a different, more demanding need to use that time to the utmost. You come to realize that wasting time may be wasting money. You will quickly learn the difference between wasting time, spending time and investing time. Time and money are the capital you invest in achieving your financial goals. You will become more demanding of yourself, insisting that the time you invest is actually yielding results. You quickly learn how to eliminate wasted time and effort. Your goals are yours and no one else's. The same is true of your time, which must be guarded jealously if you are to attain your vision and goal of financial independence.

MBD *insights*
You and you alone are responsible for reaching your goal of financial success.

Four Types of Professional Business Development People
To maximize your effectiveness in Professional Business Development, it's helpful to know the point from which you're starting. In terms of Goal-Setting and related planning, people typically fit into one of four categories. Which best describes you?

■ There are those among us who have written goals and talk easily about these goals in specific terms. They know what their goals are, why they set them, which have been accomplished, which have not and why. They have written plans detailing their attainment of their goals, the obstacles they anticipate, and alternate plans for reaching them. They keep this information readily at hand to assist them in staying focused on day-to-day activities necessary to the execution of the plan and the attainment of their goals.

■ There are those who say, "I know what I want, but I haven't taken the time to write it down." These people generally give a vague response when asked about their goals. They know they are reaching for something, but not to the extent that it is the driving force in their professional lives. They typically say, "I'd like to..." rather than, "My goal is...". They might say, "It's my aspiration that...I hope that I will be able to...". These are individuals who aspire to achievements but haven't clearly visualized them, written them down, or committed to them. They have the drive to set goals but they have not learned the Goal-Setting process or laid plans for achieving their goals. These individuals need to dig deeper within themselves to find out if they are really goal-motivated, and, if so, specifically what they are reaching for and whether they are prepared to learn how to achieve it and to pay the price for it.

■ There are those who know goals are important, but have not been in enough pain to set them. They may be people who have reached all the goals they previously had set. Or they may have attended all the seminars and read all the books, but somehow not been challenged enough to apply the principles to themselves. If they reflect on times when they were more goal-driven, chances are they will realize that their lives were much more satisfying during those periods.

■ There are those who do not understand the how and why of being goal-driven. These people typically say, "I've made it this far without doing that," or "I like to keep my options open," or some such comment. Sometimes they laugh at others who do set goals. Deep down inside they are probably simply afraid. A small voice inside is telling them, "Don't set goals. What if you don't reach them?"

Where do you fit into this spectrum of goal-setters or non-goal-setters? Chances are you wouldn't be in the position you're in now without having set some goals – at least unspoken ones. If the idea of setting written goals is new to you, consider how much greater your accomplishments could become with the aid of clearly stated written goals. Thinking about and stating your goals this way can give new focus to your efforts and help you keep in proper perspective the various facets of your daily work. Each of you has been provided a comprehensive Goal-Setting and planning exercise as part of your initial training. By completing that self-evaluation and Goal-Setting and planning process, you commit yourself to the achievement of the goals that are important to you. It helps you keep in mind what you are working for every day.

Appropriate Goals for the Individual in the Business Development Role

What kinds of goals should you set? Certainly, you must have both personal and professional goals, and you must be able to reconcile them with each other. Of course, there's no perfect list, but at a minimum consider setting goals in the following fundamental categories:

- Family
- Financial
- Intellectual/Personal Development
- Physical
- Professional/Career
- Social
- Spiritual/Emotional

Once you have identified the types of goals you should be addressing and have set your own personal goals, the next step is to determine if there is compatibility between your goals as an individual and those that apply to your role as a Professional Business Development executive. Do you have goals in one area that conflict with goals in another area? How will you reconcile the tension? Can they be made compatible, or if you succeed in one area are you setting yourself up for failure in another? To work at an optimal level of effectiveness and to find satisfaction in your career, your personal and professional goals must be congruent.

> *To work at an optimal level of effectiveness and to find satisfaction in your career, your personal and professional goals must be congruent.*

Remember that a house divided will fall, and a person cannot serve two masters. It is fundamental that your goals in each area are complementary, and that the goals of your company are consistent with your own. Working in a situation with congruent goals makes it possible to grow from a dependent to an independent to an interdependent relationship with your organization.

What Time Frame Is Appropriate For Reaching Your Goals?

An important aspect of the Goal-Setting process is the time frame involved. You should have some means of determining your degree of success in achieving your goals, and a time frame is an effective tool. Both short-term and long-term objectives can provide the critical measurements you will need. Two good general rules are:

- Short-term goals – reachable within the current year
- Long-term goals – reachable 3 to 5 years in the future

The Measure of Meaningful Goals

Anyone can set a goal. But how does the Business Development Professional measure the appropriateness of his or her goals? What is a proper benchmark?

Of course, the individual is the best and final arbiter of this question. Only you will know whether you have truly chosen a meaningful goal for yourself, copped out with a goal that's too easy, or subconsciously set yourself up for failure. It is imperative that your Business Development goals be in harmony with your personal traits and your personal goals. Any incompatibilities should be addressed as soon as they are discovered. The differences and conflicts must be rectified in order to avoid the pitfalls of indecision and procrastination that eventually will follow and will have to be reconciled later in a much more difficult setting.

Your personal self-image will generally guide you in setting professional goals that you feel are within your realm of achievement. If you are ill at ease with what you may perceive as an overly ambitious goal, this is the time to examine the reasons for your discomfort. Goals should be challenging, but if you are inordinately antipathetic about an ambitious goal, these feelings may be prompted by your self-image. Even executives can be vulnerable to self-doubt from early experiences and their subsequent effects. A thoughtful consideration of the reasons for your reluctance will likely reflect a self-image in need of examination.

Using Your SMARTS to Set Meaningful Goals

As a senior-level manager, no doubt you've had considerable experience in setting goals for your department, or even for your company. But many executives find it more difficult to set personal goals for their own careers. How can you be sure the goals you are setting are appropriate for your work in Professional Business Development? A set of benchmarks would be helpful.

You may remember that in the Mastering Business Development® Training Workshop, we spent some time discussing a system for evaluating your goals. A useful set of benchmarks is contained in the easy-to-remember acronym SMARTS. As you move toward setting your own personal and professional goals, consider these guidelines. Are your goals:

- Specific – Any goal should be clearly defined. Can you clearly and accurately describe it? Will it be understood if read or communicated to others?

- Measurable – Do you have a quantitative means of measuring the attainment of your goal both on a short-term and long-term basis? How will you quantitatively know if you've reached it? For example, a $1,000,000 revenue goal can easily be broken down to $83,333 per month.

- Attainable – Could you or anyone reasonably expect to attain the goal? It has to be believable to be achievable. The ability to become convinced of the attainability of a goal is based on your ability to devise and implement a plan for its attainment.

- Within Your Resources – Do you have the appropriate resources available in time commitment, education and other capital to attain these goals? Do you have, within your plan, means of addressing shortcomings in resources? A goal must be evaluated in terms of the available resources and other factors that will influence your ability to achieve it.

The ability to become convinced of the attainability of a goal is based on your ability to devise and implement a plan for its attainment.

- Time-Limited – A time limit is necessary to avoid allowing goals to become simply dreams. Have you given yourself a defined amount of time to achieve your goals? There are no unreasonable goals, only unreasonable time frames.

■ Stretch-Inducing – A Goal-Setting exercise should always result in goals that force the individual to reach in order to achieve them. He or she should have to reach externally and aspire to more, reach internally and require more.

MBD *insights*

Without goals it is difficult to succeed or measure success.

Goals should be slightly out of reach, but not out of sight. By breaking a goal down to its smallest components, you can develop an incremental approach to success. Evaluate your progress toward the goal in terms of these increments.

There are no unreasonable goals, only unreasonable time frames.

For example, is it easier for you to picture yourself selling $1,000,000 in products or services this year or making seven phone calls today? By implementing a system that measures these smaller steps of the process, it is easier to recognize when you are off-target and make corrections.

It is absolutely essential that you track your progress on a daily basis. At the end of each day, week, month, year, you must be able to say, "I did well." And you must evaluate your work by measuring your behavior – not your results. Be assured that if your behavior is consistent and goal-oriented, results will follow.

Another fundamental element that must be in your goal-achievement system is rewarding yourself along the way. Don't wait to reward yourself only for the big sale. By the time it gets here you may be long dead from burnout. Instead, reward yourself for completing small steps along the way.

Inside each of us there is a little person who does not like discomfort and will go to great lengths to avoid it. If your goal is to make 20 cold calls per day, no matter how dedicated you are, you will probably not look forward to making them. It will be easier to do "more productive" things, such as sharpening your pencils, straightening the items on your desk or handling the mail. Use these easier tasks as rewards. Make a deal with the little person inside that as soon as you complete your calls, you can check your e-mail.

If your behavior is consistent and goal-oriented, results will follow.

Goal-Setting and Motivation

Virtually every theory of motivation is based on the premise that all motivation is self-motivation. More than most fields, Business Development is a self-managing profession driven by goals, not controls. Goals, then, become a tangible expression of what motivates you as a Business Development Professional.

Business Development is a self-managing profession driven by goals, not controls.

Most motivation theories hold that human energy stems from internal needs. Consequently, the purpose of motivated behavior is to reduce tension in the individual through satisfying those needs.

Let's look at a few of these theories in the context of Goal-Setting:

The Path-Goal Theory

The Path-Goal Theory suggests that people will behave in a manner that will lead to the attainment of a goal which they value – and which they believe they can achieve. Three criteria are essential:

- Goal Availability – The goals they want to achieve must be available within the context of the organization for which they work. There must be a match between their goals and the organization's goals.

- Good Value – The rewards offered by the organization for achieving the goals must be of value to them.

- Perceived Effort-Reward Probability – They must believe that a given amount and type of effort (such as executing a Business Development system) will result in the attainment of their goals.

Maslow's Hierarchy of Needs Theory

Maslow's Hierarchy of Needs Theory holds that people must satisfy lower-level needs (physical, security and social) before focusing on the higher needs of self-esteem and self-actualization. Maslow points out two factors that particularly relate to Goal-Setting:

- Our natural desire is to seek the higher-level goals.

- Self-actualization is the one need we can never fully satisfy. Even as we approach that level, setting and achieving ever-higher goals can continue to drive our activity.

Herzberg's Dual Factory Theory

Herzberg's Dual Factor Theory identifies two basic job dimensions:

- Job Context – This includes administrative policy, working conditions, compensation and benefits, interpersonal relations, type of management and the like.

- Job Content – This includes the sense of achievement, challenge and recognition that comes from the work itself.

All these theories agree that performance improves when it is motivated by believable and achievable goals that result in valued rewards. From a Goal-Setting perspective, then, motivation can be seen as:

- The ability to see in a present action a projection of the future you want for yourself. You must be able to see what you are doing right now in the context of your goals. Otherwise, you are not motivated to do it. You're simply doing as you're told.

- Putting a plan into motion. It must be a plan that you believe will actually achieve what you really want in the future.

- Being aware of the investment you must pay to achieve your plan. Once aware, you must be willing to pay that price.

- Recognizing movement toward your goal on a daily basis. The motivational speaker Robert Schuller is often quoted as saying, "Yard by yard, life is hard. Inch by inch, it's a cinch." Nowhere is this more true than in Professional Business Development.

The Motivation Formula

Motivation theories can be complex and unfriendly. Often, it helps to reduce a complex concept down to a simple – probably overly simple – formula. For example, the following formula may be helpful to you as you seek to understand motivation and Goal-Setting:

Motivation = (D + A + K)

D = Dissatisfaction (either internal or external)
A = Awareness of the desired result/expectation
K = Knowledge of how to get there

It means simply that motivation stems from dissatisfaction plus awareness of the desired result and knowledge of how to reach that result. D, Dissatisfaction, or need, drives "what is." But that is not enough to result in motivated behavior. We must also be (A) aware of "what should be" in terms of what we desire and what we expect our action to produce. These two factors provide us with a motivation gap. To close that gap, we must have one more ingredient: K, knowledge of how to get there. Knowing what is and what should be is just another way of describing Goal-Setting. Goals define the present and the future, and they establish a framework for daily action. As professionals in Business Development, we will find that our success with Goal-Setting will be inextricably linked to our motivation.

Unlike your purpose of helping your clients meet their needs, your goals are strictly self-centered. What do you want to attain and why?

Additional Goal-Setting Suggestions

For many professionals in Business Development, becoming convinced of the need for Goal-Setting is far easier than actually setting goals. Successful Goal-Setting requires the use of many varied techniques and tools. Here are some additional tips, garnered from the many participants in our workshops over the years, that will help guarantee your success in setting your goals.

- You must write down your goals. It's hard to let yourself off the hook for not accomplishing written goals. It's also wise to write down each week the behavior necessary to progress during that week toward the attainment of your goals.

- Anticipate obstacles. Identify and have a plan to circumvent any potential obstacles that would thwart your progress toward your goal. Once you have identified your obstacles, consider an alternate plan you will follow when you encounter them. You have given up excuses for failure.

- Have resources available. Identify what's required in terms of people, equipment, tools and time and be prepared to secure any resource necessary to achieve your goal.

- Plan for additional education and training. Anticipate the need to gain new knowledge and skills that will be necessary to achieve your goals. It's your responsibility.

- Develop a system that enables you to create and track a plan of action. Be sure you know how you can measure the degree of your success.

- Ask, "What's in it for me?" Be able to answer that question relative to each of your personal goals. Remember that your goals in Professional Business Development are necessarily selfish. Unlike your purpose of helping your clients meet their needs, your goals are strictly self-centered. What do you want to attain and why?

The Focusing Benefits of Goal-Setting

Without a clear vision of your goal, it's difficult to become excited about achieving it. And it's difficult to know when you have achieved it. A well-defined and recognized goal can bring your life into focus in areas that otherwise would be lacking this attribute. The consummate executives have their goals in focus and are making a continued effort to bring them into reality in both a personal and a professional venue. Goal-Setting can strengthen your ability to stay focused and to use effectively one of the most valuable of all assets – time.

Goal-Setting, in fact, functions as a sort of magnifying glass through which to view the day's activities. Setting goals will help you work better in ways you may not have thought of. Consider these valuable by-products of Goal-Setting that can help you reach your overall goal of becoming more effective in Business Development. Setting goals:

> *The consummate executives have their goals in focus and are making a continued effort to bring them into reality in both a personal and a professional venue.*

■ *Will help you improve your self-esteem.* A sense of accomplishment is an enriching by-product of all stages of goal achievement. Knowing where you are going and what steps you've already taken on the path can do wonders for the way you see yourself.

■ *Will help you improve your career performance.* Focusing on your goals and the steps necessary to reach them eliminates wasted time and effort and channels energy more productively. It simply stimulates you to get to your goals as quickly as possible. You will push yourself to work harder and smarter.

■ *Makes you aware of your strengths.* Goal-Setting helps you become more aware of your strengths in overcoming obstacles and providing solutions for problems. Recognizing your strengths helps to focus your goals and capitalize on those strengths.

■ *Helps you recognize your successes.* Goal achievement provides moments to be celebrated, then stimulates new achievement. As you reward yourself for incremental steps along the way, you will be increasingly motivated to set even higher goals. Success breeds success.

■ *Focuses your daily activities.* Goal-Setting and achievement involve step-by-step accomplishment of daily activities designed to achieve your goals. Goals give you a methodical approach to your daily activity culminating in achievement. Without them, daily activities become simply busy work, lacking purpose and resulting in no accomplished results.

■ *Helps you separate reality from wishful thinking.* If you're committed to achieving a specific goal, you'll establish a realistic time line and plan for its achievement. If you're a daydreamer, a fuzzier view will do. You probably won't bother.

■ *Recognize and strengthen your weaknesses.* A wise person once said, "Our weaknesses remain weaknesses until we do something about them." By setting and working toward our goals, we become aware of our weaknesses and our challenge to address them. Without the habit of setting and attaining goals, we remain ignorant of the limitations that hold us back. Our limitations are limitations only as long as we allow them to be.

Our limitations are limitations only as long as we allow them to be.

■ *Set a life course and accept responsibility.* By daring to set a life course, you will clarify your values, beliefs, attitudes, priorities and necessary behaviors. Goal-Setting separates you from those who have not accepted responsibility for their lives. This clarification makes it easier to discipline yourself to perform the behaviors necessary for success.

By choosing to enter the process of setting and pursuing goals, you have forced yourself into the position of accepting responsibility for your own life.

You have come to realize that you alone bear the responsibility for making your life a model of success and satisfaction, both personally and profession-ally. Would you have it any other way?

"Nothing astonishes men so much as common sense and plain dealing...If the single man plant himself indomitable on his instincts, and there abide, the huge world will come round to him."

—Ralph Waldo Emerson

6

Psychology for the Business Development Professional:

People Knowledge, Knowing Yourself and Others

There is no more valuable or relevant skill available to the Business Development Professional than the capacity to understand basic human psychology – people skills. Although our discussion here can only scratch the surface of such a broad area of study, it can arm you with the tools you need to understand the behavior of two very important people: your customer or prospect and, even more importantly, yourself.

Since 60 percent of the reasons for Business Development failure can be defined as conceptual, it is of the utmost importance to be able to recognize and deal with these difficulties. This chapter will help you examine your own conceptual limitations and give you some insights on how to deal with them.

The literature of psychology, of course, is broad and complex. For our purposes, an especially helpful approach is found in the concepts and principles of Transactional Analysis, put forward by the late Dr. Eric Berne. Transactional Analysis (TA) promotes the understanding of human behavior through analyzing interactions, or transactions, between human beings. These ideas were presented by Dr. Berne in several books, the earliest of which was *Games People Play.* Dr. Berne's focus includes these important points:

■ People develop life positions based on their conditioning through early experiences. These lead to perceptions of themselves and others as either being OK or Not OK.

■ Personality is composed and expressed predominantly from three Ego States: Parent, Adult and Child.

■ By understanding the messages and conditioning of these three Ego States and the transactions that take place between individuals in terms of these Ego States, human interactions can be improved.

Our material and techniques in this area are based on TA because a workable, basic understanding of yourself and others is essential in successful Business Development. It behooves the Business Development Professional to do some outside reading over a period of years on the subject of psychology in general and TA in particular.

A workable, basic understanding of yourself and others is essential in successful Business Development.

A good entry-level, easily understandable book is *Born to Win* by Muriel James and Dorothy Jongeward. It offers a basic introduction to Structural Analysis and includes exercises in Gestalt therapy to help individuals understand the source of their conditioning. Other entry-level reading might include *I'm OK - You're OK* or *Staying OK* by Thomas Harris, and *Egograms* by John Dusay.

For more advanced reading, we recommend *In and Out of the Garbage Pail* by Frederick Perls, who originated Gestalt therapy. *Scripts People Live* by Claude Steiner offers insight into typical scripts played out by many of us throughout life, along with *Politics of the Family* by R.D. Laing and *Psycho-Cybernetics* by Maxwell Maltz.

Dr. Berne's two other classics, *What Do You Say After You Say Hello?* and his popularized *Games People Play*, include all his clinical material in a non-professional application.

MBD *insights*

The first person you must understand is yourself.

Life Positions: OK or Not OK

The chief reason Business Development Professionals find it difficult to operate with an attitude of accomplishment is that they feel fundamentally insecure. They really don't feel good about being in this profession. While Business Development people are especially vulnerable to the effects of their insecurities, they're not the only ones who feel this way about their work and themselves. Everyone faces much the same experiences that, left unexamined, can lead to feelings of inferiority and insecurity. Beginning at birth, each of us learns that in many ways we are not "good enough," and we tend to think that everyone else is more intelligent, more accomplished, or more important somehow.

Dr. Berne's principles of psychology teach that there are two ways people can feel about themselves: OK or Not OK. Feelings of OKness come from being assured and confident in various situations and could be described to include safety, contentment, happiness, security, comfort, satisfaction or credibility. Not OK feelings would be reflective of insecurity and lack of confidence and may include such emotions as dissatisfaction, unhappiness, confusion, inferiority, tension, fear or loneliness.

There are two ways people can feel about themselves: OK or Not OK.

Dr. Berne's material proposes that 98 percent of the population would choose to feel OK if given a choice between feeling OK or Not OK. The remaining 2 percent he describes as those suffering from various types of mental problems that cause them to prefer feeling Not OK. Remarkably, however, of the 98 percent who would choose OKness, only about 3 percent actually feel OK on a frequent basis. A residual 95 percent, most of the time, see themselves as Not OK, or to some degree insecure.

Transactional Analysis purports that people acquire four fundamental "life positions" in early childhood that continue to shape behavior throughout life. These interactive positions are:

■ I'm OK – You're OK – The perception that each person is of equal value, with the feeling of giving and receiving the mutual respect of human dignity. The healthiest of the four positions.

■ I'm OK – You're Not OK – This is manifested by individuals who suffer from a deep-seated inferiority complex based on inferior feelings of self-worth. Early in life these people have usually had traumatic experiences, often including childhood abuse. These individuals later in life find it necessary to obtain a feeling of OKness by making others feel Not OK, and they are often abusive of others, quite often to the extreme. Typical examples include murderers, rapists, and those who overtly abuse others. History provides us abundant examples of the fascist totalitarian dictator who victimizes innocent people.

- I'm Not OK – You're OK – This is a frequently held position by an unusually high number of people, quite often those in Business Development. We will look at the reasons for this later. In this position the individual sees himself as less important or less worthwhile than others. This position is characterized by an individual's reluctance to interact and by his exhibiting Not OK feelings if forced to do so.

- I'm Not OK – You're Not OK – This is a relatively small percentage of people who seek social solace from others who also feel Not OK. It is the mutual misery group. They feel good by feeling bad and commiserating about it. Since they feel Not OK, they believe other people are like them. Those afflicted with addiction to drugs or alcohol are usually in this group, though it certainly includes others as well. They find comfort in socializing with people like themselves who feel Not OK, and they operate from that life position. Gloom, pessimism, destructiveness and dejection are indicators of this consortium. Frequently victims of a dysfunctional social environment in their childhood, they learn to value neither themselves nor others. Their outlook is completely pessimistic and destructive.

Why Do We Feel Not OK?

How do most of us come to believe, most of the time, that we are Not OK? The process begins at birth.

Think about it. Before you're born, you're completely warm and protected, carried around in your mother's body, fed constantly without ever feeling hungry. Then comes birth – not an easy experience. The room you come into is cold. Soon the doctor is spanking your bottom, and from there it gets worse. They take you home, and a long series of "no" messages begin to replace the unspoken "yes" messages you've been used to.

Everyone else seems to go to the bathroom okay. No problem. But you're different. Soon, you're seated at the dining table. Everyone else eats with a knife and fork, pretty accomplished. What do you do? After dinner, they clean you up and put you back in the playpen (prison) for a few hours. You're smaller than everyone else, you can't do things right, you're generally a mess. Each of us by about age 6 has acquired plenty of reasons to feel Not OK, even if we're brought up in the ideal family. The situation of helplessness itself is enough to make us feel Not OK.

Each of us by about age 6 has acquired plenty of reasons to feel Not OK.

In his book, *The Brain*, Dr. Richard Restak writes that our brains are capable of storing more information than is contained in all the libraries in the world. Dr. Restak explains that the conscious mind investigates and interprets all the experiences we encounter. This is accomplished by the use of all five of our senses: hearing, sight, smell, taste and touch. These experiences of the conscious mind are soon forgotten, mostly because of the necessity of dealing consistently and consecutively with new experience. Because our mind deals only in "real time," handling one experience after another, we soon forget what is stored there.

In the subconscious mind, however, is recorded and stored all our conscious input. These include our thoughts, feelings and observations as they are experienced. It is much like a large-capacity hard disk in a computer. It stores whatever is presented to it at the time and does not interpret or evaluate the information.

It's understandable, then, that whatever is stored in the subconscious mind continually surfaces to influence our conscious thoughts. These thoughts shape our daily actions, and these actions become mental and behavioral habits that are themselves stored in the subconscious mind.

The Not OKness that begins to creep into our thought processes from birth creates a lot of false information about us. And because the subconscious mind has recorded and stored this misinformation as fact, it keeps surfacing to shape our actions and form our mental and behavioral habits.

To understand how this subconscious record of Not OKness can influence our lives, let's consider the concept of a Life Script, one of the fundamental tenets of Transactional Analysis that has been explained by Claude Steiner. In his book, *Scripts People Live*, Steiner says that people are conditioned to one of two types of scripts in life – either banal or tragic scripts. They spend much of their lives acting out the behavior that is implied by their scripts, which are their subconscious record of attitudes, beliefs, values and feelings since childhood. People become psychologically conditioned to function from either an OK or a Not OK position. Those with a tragic life script will assume that they and others are equally Not OK, or they will see themselves as OK and others as Not OK.

Most of us rarely encounter individuals with tragic life scripts, although history has provided us classic examples of them. Much more common to each of us is the banal life script, which typically says, "Play it safe in the world. Live up to other people's expectations." These are people who "died at 30 and are buried somewhere past 60." They typically feel powerless over their own lives and are frequently heard making statements from their scripts such as, "I wish we had...If only...Sometime we might...Life's not fair...If I had my life to live over...." These are people who generally struggle through life, quite often without Goals and Plans. They see themselves as part of other peoples' plans, quite often as victims, and think there is little they can do to change their situation. They typically lead lives of quiet desperation, never completely giving up on themselves, yet never fulfilling their full capabilities.

Each of us has the capacity to change our life scripts, but we must recognize that all of us are scripted early in life to operate in a certain way. Many of us operate from a banal script that typically perceives the other individual as being more OK and ourselves being somewhat Not OK. Recognizing the injunctions and attributions that we are given early in life that make up our life script is critical. Our ability to change those messages and bring about the life we wish is a challenge, both personally and professionally.

Recognizing the injunctions and attributions that we are given early in life that make up our life script is critical. Our ability to change those messages and bring about the life we wish is a challenge, both personally and professionally.

Implications for Business Development

What does all this mean for the Business Development Professional? Why should you care about psychology? For one very good reason: It is absolutely essential for your success.

Why? Because of this fundamental truth. Remember we said earlier that 98 percent of people want to feel OK, but only about 3 percent do? This means that 95 percent of people, most of the time, are feeling Not OK and searching for a way to feel OK. And the most common way to gain the feeling of OKness is to convince yourself that someone else is more Not OK than you are.

The implications for Professional Business Development are profound. Consider this example: You're Charlie Pro, the hottest thing to hit Business Development this year. You drive up to the front of a company where you will make your business call. You hop out in your pinstripe suit, 12-pound wingtips, Gucci briefcase, and pocket full of Mont Blanc pens. You look good, sound good, walk in and meet the receptionist.

She's already had a difficult morning. The kids were slow getting ready for school, so she was late. And she earns barely enough to make working worthwhile. She's sitting there wondering why she didn't take her father's advice and go to college and become a nurse. And you walk in, looking like a million bucks. She figures you earn eight or ten times her salary. She's feeling Not OK. The way you look makes her feel even more Not OK.

You tell her you'd like to see the president. She says icily, "Do you have an appointment? No? Well, of course, he doesn't see anyone without an appointment." She has made you feel Not OK now. So much for the flashy clothes. You slink out the door in your wingtips, and, sure enough, she feels better.

Or say by some miracle you do get past the receptionist and are sitting in front of the president. Today he's feeling a bit Not OK, too. His son called home from college to say he's overdrawn his bank account. His daughter is failing 10th grade math. And things aren't quite right between him and his wife. She's stopped buying his clothes, and his wardrobe is getting a little shabby. This morning he was too busy to polish his wingtips, and even if they were polished, they'd only weigh 10 pounds.

You look a little too good. On top of that, because you're somewhat intimidated, feeling Not OK yourself, you launch into a traditional presentation of the features and benefits of your product or service. You do what we call "spilling your candy in the lobby." You tell him more than he ever wanted to know, including the fact that your product will solve some problems he doesn't even understand. You look very confident, and you're feeling like things are going pretty well.

What is he thinking? I'm not buying from this guy. I'll cut him down a notch or two. At the end of your stellar presentation, he says in his most condescending manner, "Do you have a card? I'll give you a call."

These are typical examples of Lose/Lose business transactions. You may have looked OK to the receptionist, but inside you were feeling vulnerable. The unpleasant task of making initial calls dipped deep into your subconscious mind and unearthed a lot of Not OK information. This was strongly reinforced by the receptionist's parent-to-child type of greeting. By the time you got to the president, you felt uneasy enough to take refuge in your traditional presentation, which gave you something to say instead of, "I'm scared. Please say you like me."

Buying is generally a Not OK experience.

As long as your Not OK feelings cause you to "look for love in all the wrong places," you will remain a vulnerable child in each new Business Development situation.

Both you and your prospect are using the situation to get your emotional needs met. You lose the business opportunity, and you leave feeling even more Not OK. The customer loses the potential benefit he could have obtained from your product or service.

Remember that buying is generally a Not OK experience for your customer. He has to spend money, which is an unpleasant prospect. But before that, he has to realize he has a problem – one he may not be sure how to solve. Maybe your product will solve it, and maybe it won't. The uncertainties of the situation make your customer feel Not OK.

Being "sold" is a Not OK

If you are very forceful in dictating a solution, you will intensify the customer's Not OK feelings. Being "sold" is a Not OK feeling, and your client will strive to feel OK by resisting and cutting you down. To change a business transaction to a Win/Win situation, you must help your client feel OK and encourage the wisdom of his decision to buy a solution to his problem.

Structural Analysis: The Three Ego States

Let's look a little closer at the dynamics of interpersonal transactions. Just as TA explains the psychological interactions between two people, Structural Analysis (SA) is the psychological understanding of one person. It can be applied to yourself or to another, and it can be useful in predicting behavior. It requires identification of the "Ego State" from which one person is operating. In every personality there are what Dr. Eric Berne called three Ego States: Parent, Adult and Child. Think of these as three directories of the "hard disk" of your brain. When the information in any one of these directories on the disk is in control of your actions, you will act in a certain way based on that information. When the Parent, Adult and Child Ego States in an individual are not relatively balanced, and often they are not, one Ego State becomes dominant in influencing both the intellectual and emotional behaviors.

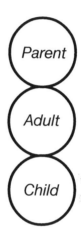

We analogized the three Ego States in computer vernacular as the hard disk of the brain. Each Ego State has individual stored information separate from the others, and behavior is affected by the influence of the information from one or more of these Ego States. This information within each directory is placed there in early childhood, the majority between birth and six years of age. And, just as much of the information on a real computer's hard disk is hidden from the user, much of the information in your Parent, Adult and Child directories is hidden from you in the subconscious mind. By using Transactional Analysis to examine and understand how this information got there, you can uncover these hidden messages and discover why you – and your clients – act the way you do.

These three Ego States, or directories, are not typically the same size in each person. Their size and strength in defining behavior depends on the individual's upbringing and early experiences. At any time, an individual is operating from only one of the three Ego States. With practice you will begin to recognize the Ego State you are acting or reacting from and begin to have control over your behavior as it affects other individuals.

MBD *insights*

At any given time, an individual operates from only one Ego State.

Let's look first at the Parent section of your "disk."

Information on the Parent directory of your disk came from external sources – your father, mother, grandparents, older siblings, doctors, policemen, clergy and other authority figures. Most of the information was placed there by the time you were six. On this directory of your disk is some interesting information that you have probably absorbed without ever thinking about it. Parent information includes injunctions –"dos and don'ts" – and attributions about other people that often come out as prejudices. It includes useful information, from how to tie your shoes to how to stack the laundry. It includes a lot of "ifs"– stated or implied directives that said "I'll love you if..." you make good grades, don't bother me, or whatever. And it includes everything you heard about your heritage and traditions.

The Parent Ego State can be subdivided into two, usually unequal, parts: Critical Parent and Nurturing Parent. The Critical Parent is arbitrary and judgmental, offering criticism, discipline and boundaries of behavior. Examples: "Tie your shoes...Don't bother your father when he's busy...Put that down if you don't want a spanking." These compromising and negatively reinforced examples, and many others that most of us can recall from childhood, are retained throughout life in the Parent Ego State directory in our brain's hard disk. They call into question the motives for one's behavior and consequently restrict it. The Critical Parent is important for Business Development Professionals in two ways: in the Professional Business Development environment, if the attitudes acquired from the Critical Parent input are not checked, they can result in a reluctance to make cold calls and a propensity to take any rejection – even on a strictly business basis – as personal. Also, if you exhibit the overbearing nature of the Critical Parent and appear authoritative, pushy or demanding with your clients, you will certainly be met with rejection.

The Parent Ego State can be subdivided into two, usually unequal, parts: Critical Parent and Nurturing Parent.

Consider these messages you may remember from your own Critical Parent tape: "Don't play with the phone...it's not a toy. Never talk to strangers. Your father (or some other adult) is busy...don't bother him." How will these messages make you feel about making Business Development calls? Chances are, you'll be one of the walking wounded who does a lot of "getting ready to get ready" before making a call. Your basic attitudes, beliefs, and values are in conflict with what you're being asked to do in a role. Then, if you are turned down rudely, you're likely to take it personally and go into Afterburn, which means it will be almost impossible for you to make another call.

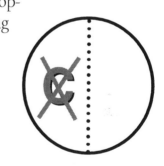

THE CRITICAL PARENT

And there's the other important factor of the Critical Parent from the Business Development perspective. Critical Parent behavior is perceived as pushy, authoritative and overbearing, and always brings resistance from those who perceive it. If you are not careful, the traditional "features and benefits" barrage of information you deliver to your clients will come across as Critical Parent behavior. The client will go along with you until he or she gets a chance to get even by turning you down.

MBD *insights*

Zero percent of successful Business Development comes from the Critical Parent.

The derivative of the Parent Ego State that is beneficial to Business Development is the Nurturing Parent. The Nurturing Parent is the warm, receptive portion that is empathetic, whether or not it is sympathetic. It offers empathy and infusion of feelings to others. It furthers the development of an understanding and sensitivity toward others through an awareness and recognition of their feelings. It's the part of your personality that has the capacity to be externally focused and generally concerned with the betterment of the other person.

The Nurturing Parent educates, understands, assists, advises, guides and develops, all in a gentle and almost unconditional manner. The eclectic traits of the Nurturing Parent are acquired from role models, older and kindly relatives, teachers and others. The behavior of the Nurturing Parent tends to ask questions, listen and stay low-key. It is the kind uncle, aunt, grandmother, grandfather, mentor, coach or role model. The Nurturing Parent says, "Tell me where it hurts...Let me make it better...Go ahead. I'll bet you can do it." In Business Development, this is the part of your personality

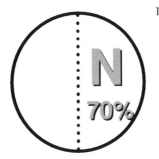

THE NURTURING PARENT

that actually tries to help your clients or prospects. It is the part that focuses on their problem and their situation from their perspective. It tends to be empathetic and allows your prospects to feel comfortable in sharing with you their concerns and problems.

MBD *insights*

Seventy percent of successful Business Development behavior comes from the Nurturing Parent.

Child Ego State

While the Critical Parent can cause some problems for the Business Development Professional, it is the Child Ego State that quite often is the most troublesome. Most of the information on the Child directory of your hard disk is placed there between birth and six years of age. It is information that came from sources internal to you. Each individual is born with the physical capacity to feel, but each of us is taught how we should feel. In some situations we encounter early in life, we receive messages from other people on whether we should feel OK or Not OK. Regrettably, much of the information we receive is negative and presents a general aura of Not OKness. The Child Ego State presents the most problems for the Business Development Professional. It is composed of three divisions: the Adaptive Child, the Rebellious Child and the Natural Child. Each division can be an asset or a liability.

The Adaptive Child is the part of your personality that does whatever is necessary to get what is perceived as parental approval. If early parental approval is absent, unexpressed, or conditional, it may result in the development of an oversized Adaptive Child who harbors characteristics of conformity and fear. The presence of these traits can create obstacles to successful Business Development, particularly in the area of initiative.

To risk what is perceived as rejection and make initial cold contacts is very difficult for those who possess a very large Adaptive Child. As we discussed earlier, there must be a separation of roles in a situation like this. Self-worth is not at stake here, and only the emotionally healthy person who has separated the professional and personal roles can endure the rejection that is attendant to the role of the Business Development Professional. Only an emotionally healthy person who realizes his or her self-worth does not depend on success in the role of Business Development will be able to survive the daily rejections that are part of this role. Without having made this separation, the individual will be vulnerable to a shattering of the ego that will raise the floodgate on the reservoir of Not OKness already present. Initial contact calls will soon be out of the question, and failure will be certain.

The Child Ego State presents the most problems for the Business Development Professional.

THE CHILD

It's often jokingly said that when traditional Business Development Professionals are born, the doctor leaves an unnaturally long umbilical cord. Instead of an "inny" or an "outy," they get a "longy." Then they spend the rest of their lives looking for a place to plug it back in. "Mr. Customer, will you love me?" is their message, rather than "How can I help you?" The implications for failure in Business Development are obvious. You cannot go into Business Development to get your emotional needs met. Failure will be swift and certain.

MBD *insights*

You cannot go into Business Development expecting to meet your emotional needs.

In the Professional Business Development arena, an unchecked Child Ego State that is overconditioned can result in devastation. The characteristics of the Adaptive Child must be deleted from any professional business interaction.

An equally useless part of the Child Ego State is what's called the Rebellious Child. The Rebellious Child resents the power of the parent and says, "So what?" This trait is normal, and it's acceptable as long as the individual takes the action by choice. But it also can be destructive when someone else is pulling the individual's strings – when the individual lets himself or herself be manipulated into behavior because of old and inappropriate information in the Rebellious Child Ego State. For example, a Business Development Professional may have an oversized Rebellious Child because during his early upbringing he was treated in an extremely authoritative manner. If a customer begins to behave in what he perceives to be the Critical Parent style, it will be difficult for the Business Development Professional to resist slipping into the Rebellious Child mode and playing "Up yours" with the customer. And one game of "Up yours" will probably be enough to destroy any potential for future sales.

The Adaptive Child is the part of your personality that does whatever is necessary to get what is perceived as parental approval.

The third aspect of the Child Ego State, however, can be quite helpful to the Business Development Professional. This is the Natural Child, sometimes called "Curious George" or the "Little Professor." This is the free, effervescent six-year-old inside each of us, the part that always wants to know why and how. It's the natural curiosity that children have, extended into adulthood. The Natural Child Ego State develops to become a useful part of every adult. Each of us retains a degree of our Natural Child, and Business Development Professionals with a large Natural Child have a wonderful curiosity about people, business, and business problems. They do unusually well in Business Development. They are not embarrassed to ask a lot of seemingly dumb questions about the client's business because they are simply eager to understand how things work. This approach has a dual advantage. It helps the customer feel OK as he or she dispenses knowledge while actually providing the Business Developer with the critical information that will provide a match between his product and the client's needs. Often by the time he produces the match, he has also produced a comfortable, OK client who feels confident enough to make a buying decision.

The Adult Ego State

The Adult Ego State of your personality hard disk is the part that is growing today. It is primarily analytical and quantitative. Helpful information in the

Adult Ego State began being placed at about 8 months of age and is still being developed throughout life. It takes in information, analyzes it, and makes decisions based on fact, history and data. It asks common-sense questions and accepts the information at face value without emotional coloring. The Adult Ego State is not prejudicial, but makes decisions based on logic and objective information.

It is the part of your personality that operates from the "I think" versus the "I feel" or "I should" basis. It is the Adult Ego State that has stored on it the appropriate questions to ask that drive the Business

Development process. It is the Nurturing Parent Ego State that controls the manner the questions are asked.

MBD *insights*

About 30 percent of Professional Business Development comes from the Adult Ego State.

Reachback and Afterburn

The negative impact of a Critical Parent combined with that of a Not OK Child presents the possibility of two very troublesome emotional states for the Business Development Professional. These are known as Reachback and Afterburn.

Reachback occurs when an upcoming event begins to have an effect on your present behavior. This is a feeling of impending doom that has little or no relationship to reality. You may find yourself accepting the worst possible scenario without any factual basis as the inevitable conclusion to a situation you face. If you find yourself confronted by Reachback, remember:

MBD *insights*

Worry is interest paid in advance on borrowed trouble.

The antidote for Reachback and its accompanying state of worry is to exercise adult logical planning. In the Business Development environment, this involves planning your call in detail. This includes setting a specific goal for the call, putting together an appropriate plan, determining where you are in your Business Development process and scripting how you will execute the call.

Afterburn occurs when a past event continues to affect your behavior. For example, an unpleasant encounter with a senior prospect that caused you to be referred to a lower-level purchasing person may cause you to feel intimidated. This reflects the effects of the Not OK Child and Critical Parent Ego States. The Afterburn from this situation can result in a paralyzing reluctance to direct your calls to top management in future situations.

Reachback occurs when an upcoming event begins to have an effect on your present behavior.

To overcome Afterburn, briefly and objectively analyze the encounter, come to a logical understanding with yourself of what took place, and then move on. The next challenge, in all likelihood, will have a different and unrelated set of circumstances. These two psychological limitations must be avoided if the Business Development Professional is to succeed. The apprehension of the next call, coupled with the relapse from the last one, if not realistically understood and dealt with, will quickly lead to failure.

Pulling It All Together

What does this all mean for the Business Development Professional? Why should you concern yourself with psychology? Because of this rule: Behavior is the true measure of a person's intent. To be successful in Professional Business Development, you must be able to understand and control your own behavior and to deal with other peoples behavior in a manner that creates a balance of your Goals and Purpose. Professional skills and techniques can be learned, but the psychological and emotional impediments of our Child and Parent Ego States must be extracted. There is no place in successful Business Development for these limitations.

Behavior is the true measure of a person's intent.

You can never control another person's behavior. You can only control your reaction to it. And your reaction can influence the other person's behavior. Oftentimes, a Business Development person brings with him on a call that insecure, frightened, undisciplined six-year-old Not OK Child he carries inside. Frequently the customer brings his Child along as well. Each of you is looking for stroking that is unlikely to be coming from the other. The two of you are soon locked into a quagmire of needs that leaves the purpose of the meeting lost under the debris of this exercise. You have allowed the meeting to turn into a probable Lose/Lose situation culminating in Not OKness for both of you.

The best way to react to the inevitable feelings of Not OKness that are concomitant with a career in Business Development is not to react at all.

To be successful at Professional Business Development, you must learn to leave your Child out of this encounter. The best way to react to the inevitable feelings of Not OKness that are concomitant with a career in Business Development is not to react at all. By operating from your Adult Ego State you can exercise a larger degree of control over your behavior and control these intimidating symptoms of emotional vulnerability. The characteristics of your Adult and Nurturing Parent can then be used to lead your client to a buying decision. All of this can best be achieved by operating from a developed Adult Ego State, remembering that you are not in Professional Business Development to meet your emotional needs. Success or failure in Business Development has nothing to do with your worth as a person. Your Goals in the role of Business Development are strictly financial, and as you balance your Goals with your Purpose of helping your prospects meet their needs, even at your own emotional expense, those prospects will help you meet your Goals.

You are not in Professional Business Development to meet your emotional needs. Success or failure in Business Development has nothing to do with your worth as a person.

7

Understanding Why People Buy

An experienced pediatrician tells a story that offers a valuable insight into Business Development.

For years, the mothers of many of his patients would bring their kids in for checkups because they "had no appetite." Almost invariably, he'd check the kids and they would be healthy, sometimes even overweight. Why, then, did the mothers complain that they wouldn't eat?

One day, while he watched his wife and young son at mealtime, the answer came. Two-year-old Johnny was more interested in making designs with the food than eating it. His mother was nearing her wit's end. "Johnny!" she shrieked. "I've spent hours cooking this food. The least you can do is eat it."

"Suddenly it hit me," said the doctor. "The mother takes care of the child because she loves him. Feeding him is an expression of her love. And refusing to eat is rejection."

The parallel in the world of Business Development is all too common. How often do we catch ourselves feeling this way with a prospect? After all, we've invested a great deal of time and effort in developing him as a prospect – doing some degree of qualification, making several calls, contacts and follow-ups, only to prepare for a presentation, hopefully one that dazzles him with a series of features and benefits, most of which we believe are important to the prospect. At this point, we're convinced the prospect ought to buy.

In fact, how can he not buy from us? It seems self-evident in our minds.

Often, we forget the obvious. Just like a child, who knows when and how much he needs to eat, our prospects make their buying decisions from their own perspectives, not ours. All individuals, including our prospects, are basically self-centered. They make decisions for their reasons, never ours. For the most part, they are not really concerned about us, nor our product or service. They don't really care how much we know or how intelligent we are or what we believe. They only care fundamentally about themselves, their needs, their problems and what they believe we may or may not be able to do for them.

To become a Professional Business Partner, one of the top 3 percent of Professionals in Business Development, you must begin to understand why people buy. You may have come to think that what you want to know is how to sell, but that is not the heart of the matter. The fundamental, most critical question is why do people buy – and what motivates them to purchase from you?

Pain: The First Cause

Fundamentally, people purchase things for only one basic reason: they are in pain. If you remember nothing but this concept from reading this series, you will be well on your way to success in Business Development. People purchase things, tangible or intangible, because in their mind they feel a physical or psychological pain that they wish to relieve, or they foresee encountering a pain or problem in the future that they wish to avoid. Pain is an emotional state of mind, not an intellectual one. Pain is a negative state

People purchase things, tangible or intangible, because in their mind they feel a physical or psychological pain that they wish to relieve, or they foresee encountering a pain or problem in the future that they wish to avoid.

of mind, not a positive one. Individuals are more motivated to avoid a negative than to pursue a positive. Individuals will pursue the purchase of a product or service to avoid or overcome what they perceive in their mind as a psychological negative.

People make an emotional decision to buy. They may frequently back it up with intellectual information or rationalization. Appealing to their intellect with features and benefits information will not motivate them to buy, but understanding and addressing their emotions, helping them become aware of, take ownership of and become motivated to solve their problems will.

Consider the example of two similar television commercials by AT&T. Each is aimed at increasing long distance usage. The first commercial attempts to increase usage through a rational approach that includes a message about the percentage of savings an individual can achieve through lower rates based on time-of-day usage. Given this intellectual approach, it had little success. The second approach features a grandmotherly-looking lady on the front porch of a Midwestern farmhouse. The sun is slowly setting in the background. Our grandmother is sitting in a rocking chair, gently rocking, knitting, and a phone is sitting on a nearby table. As you approach this picture, realizing the passing of time, a nurturing, low-key voice asks, "Have you called your mother lately?" This process of engaging the prospect's emotions and eventually hooking the viewer's guilt response allows the announcer to then mention AT&T's new lower rates and associated savings based on time of day. Which of these two approaches do you believe produced the most results? The latter commercial was extremely

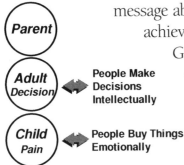

successful. People decided to buy emotionally, then justified their decision with information on the new lower rates.

Remember this rule: You can't tell and sell your prospects anything. They must decide they need it. It is far easier to get someone to buy something for their reasons than to sell them something for yours. If you try to promote the features and benefits of your product, all you are doing is pushing intellectual information to the prospect's Adult. But remember his buying decision will come from his emotional Child, not his Adult. You're aiming at the wrong target, and you will come across as an amateur, a "salesperson," engendering all the negative feelings that you associate with being "sold."

> *You can't tell and sell your prospects anything. They must decide they need it.*

Some professionals in complex, high-tech businesses still feel their customers make an intellectual decision to buy. They cite stories of prospects who compare the number of gigabytes of memory in their computers or the metallic composition of the components of a product. But if they know the solutions that their products or services provide, they'll see that the real decision to buy was made emotionally, out of a real or anticipated pain or problem, and the intellectual information was simply used as rationalization for the decision.

A story from World War II vividly illustrates how people buy emotionally to avoid pain. An enterprising individual was representing life insurance to soldiers. The policies were issued by the U.S. government, and in the event of the soldier's death, benefits would be paid by the government. When a soldier would tell the salesman, "I don't need insurance," the salesman quietly countered with a simple question.

"If you have insurance and you're killed, the government will have to pay your family $10,000. If you don't have insurance and you're killed, the government won't have to pay a dime. Think about it: If you were the government, who would you put on the front line?" The salesman sold life insurance policies as quickly as he could write them.

Risk of Change is the Key

If every buying decision is an emotional decision, then perhaps an additional question is not why people buy, but why would they risk change? Can

People will not change until the pain of change is less than the pain they are in.

you think of any purchase that does not involve the risk of change? Often a purchase involves profound changes in procedures, training, reengineering, etc. What makes a prospect willing to risk change enough to decide to buy from you? Evidence shows that people risk change because they are dissatisfied,

uncomfortable or fed up with the status quo. Again, the focus of the change is pain. People will not change until the pain of change is less than the pain they are in.

The Buying Decision Formula

There is a simple formula to explain the risk of change that also explains why people buy. It goes like this:

$$(P + A + D) > ROC = Purchase$$

Here's what these terms mean:
P = Pain (Dissatisfaction)
A = Awareness of Problem (Pain)
D = Desire to Address Problem
$> ROC$ = Risk of Change

This formula simply means that if the sum of the prospect's dissatisfaction (pain), plus the awareness of the problem plus the desire to address the problem is greater than the risk of making the change, then change or purchase will take place. Helping the prospects define these variables of change gives them an opportunity to make an appropriate emotional decision supported by the facts of the situation.

Again, the catalyst in this formula is its first element, dissatisfaction or pain. This is the variable in your equation over which you have the greatest control. The pain must be present and identified before the prospect will be interested in seeking a solution or knowledge of how to acquire it. Without pain, there will be no motivation, and therefore no purchase. The formula states in a slightly different fashion the essential truth we talked about earlier: People will not change until the pain of staying the same is greater than the pain of changing.

Think for a moment about major changes in your life involving major purchases. Did you buy your first home because you fell in love with it, or because you needed more room, a yard for the kids, or a more pleasant neighborhood? Did you trade your old car in for a new one because you felt like it or because your repairs were becoming too frequent and costly? Did your company change its computer system to stay on the cutting edge of technology, or because your old system had too many limitations? Chances are, in every case, the pain of staying in your old situation became greater than the pain of changing.

What does this tell us about Professional Business Development? The implications are clear and simple: Help your prospects identify their pain. Help them become more aware of it and take ownership and develop a desire to solve it. Much like a physician, your primary task is to diagnose, quickly and accurately, the pain your prospect may be experiencing – or may soon experience. Through careful questioning, nurturing and follow-up, begin to develop that pain and its awareness and you will be well on your way to developing a mutually beneficial relationship.

Where Does it Hurt?

Take a clue from your doctor. When you have a physical problem, what does he or she ask to diagnose it? "Where does it hurt?" "How would you describe the pain?" "How long have you been having the pain?"

Ask the right type of questions to identify the strategic business issues and concerns being faced by your prospects. Learn to ask the right questions about business, money, people and technical issues, and bring to the surface pains that can be developed into personal pain for the individuals involved. When you are capable of zeroing in on this "first-person personal" pain and what key business issues affect that individual personally, you are getting into the area that will lead the prospect to an emotional decision to let you solve his or her problem.

> *When you are capable of zeroing in on this "first-person personal" pain and what key business issues affect that individual personally, you are getting into the area that will lead the prospect to an emotional decision to let you solve his or her problem.*

In your role as a Business Development Professional, you will have to call on many people who think they are well. Their assessment of their situation may or may not be correct. The key to Professional Business Development is learning how to ask a lot of "intelligent dumb" questions looking for pain. Use your best Nurturing Parent approach to ask these questions in a very helpful, sincere, honest, caring, external way. When you uncover a pain, begin to develop it. Pick at it a little, and perhaps it will grow to become a hurt. If it hurts enough, then the prospect may begin to think of himself as less well – maybe even a little sick. Then the pain might develop to the point at which it's terminal. When it gets to the terminal stage, you may have a motivated buyer. At that point, the prospect will be willing to invest his funds in order to find a solution to his problems – for his own reasons. It is necessary to understand that this process can take several calls, during which the prospect becomes comfortable enough with you to share his pain.

Are you controlling the prospect in order to force him to buy? No, not really. In fact, you can't make any prospect buy. He must ultimately discover that he will benefit from your product or service. You can only present to him what may be problems or concerns to see if he acknowledges these concerns and then give him the opportunity to decide to solve his problem with your product or service. The prospect controls his behavior and his decision to buy – not you.

You are, however, using your knowledge of human psychology to help the prospect move as close as possible to a position of wanting to buy. Consider this analogy: You go to your doctor for an annual physical. You're feeling fine. The doctor walks in and begins to ask you questions about how you feel. Everything seems fine. He takes a few X-rays, returns 10 minutes later with them and seems worried. He asks you some more detailed questions. Now you are becoming concerned.

The doctor recommends more tests in the hospital, adding that he hopes there's no problem. By now, you don't feel so well, and you're predicting the worst at the hospital.

Up to this point, has the doctor tried to dazzle you with the features and benefits of his medical knowledge? Has he tried to impress you with his credibility? No, he's simply raised some questions, expressed concern, and asked for answers to even more detailed questions. And he's convinced you you're probably pretty sick. You're more than willing to invest in more tests.

The Behavioral Model: The Concerned Physician
People are generally more willing to talk openly about their concerns or problems than about potential pleasures – if they are convinced they're talking with an individual who is sincerely interested in them and their situation.

A key distinction that marks the Business Development Professional is the diagnostic mind-set and behavioral model of a physician who focuses on the prospects' concerns, problems or discomforts instead of the dazzling array of potential solutions offered by his or her product. To become a Professional in Business Development, you must train yourself to know what pain looks like from your client's perspective in terms of the services or products they buy. What matters is not the features and benefits of the specific product or offering, but rather the problems that these features and benefits solve in the world of the prospect. Features and benefits of a product or service are rationalizations of the value of the product. The solution to problems that are provided by the features and benefits is the value that the prospect places on the product or service. To best understand this, consider what problems you have already solved for similar clients. Take the time to ask them what these problems look like from their perspective. Locate the Child-based, pain-centered problem faced by your current clients, then ask similar prospects if they are experiencing similar pains.

Learning to scout for pain takes time, patience, and the ability to be externally focused on the other individual instead of yourself. Your chief limitation will be the natural tendency to think from your own perspective rather than the client's. To help overcome that limitation, learn as much as you can about the general business problems and industry-specific problems of your prospects. Then forsake your own ego needs enough to ask questions until you understand those problems on a personal level from your prospect's point of view.

The Hierarchy of Pain

As you learn more about interviewing and assessing prospects, you will find individuals fall into one of four suspect or prospect categories. Here's how to categorize them and choose which ones to develop further:

- "Suspects" are individuals who have an intellectual interest in your product or service, but have no current pain to justify that interest. They will solicit information from you including quotations, brochures and related information. Through this process they have the capacity to use up a great deal of your valuable time simply gathering information. Later you learn that there was no real need or pain, but that they will hold onto your information until such a time as a potential problem exists. This type of individual should be maintained in a database provided marketing information to maintain contact until such time as the pain has surfaced enough to justify further contact by you.

To become a Professional in Business Development, you must train yourself to know what pain looks like from your client's perspective in terms of the services or products they buy.

- People who have pain but are unaware of it. These are individuals who are honestly ignorant of any problems that may exist within their operation or organization. Understand that people have a right to be ignorant, and they will resent having any problems pointed out to them. You have to be careful and skillful helping these individuals became aware of the pain of which they are ignorant. Helping them become aware of, uncover and take ownership of this pain will take several contacts and diagnostic interviews. Stay in contact with these individuals, show a sincere and honest interest in them and their problems, and help them discover problems of which they are unaware.

- People who have pain, are aware of it, but don't want to do anything about it right now. Your challenge with these individuals is to get them to take ownership of the problem. Typically in this situation, they have other problems that have a higher priority. Your ability to keep the concern in the forefront of their minds will help them develop a sense of urgency to address

THE PAIN FUNNEL

Suspect
Interest - No Pain
Prospect
Pain - Unaware
Prospect
Pain - Aware
Unmotivated
Prospect
Pain - Aware
Motivated To
Solve It
Qualified
Prospect

the problem. By doing this you will help them to become motivated to seek a solution. You must stay in close contact with these individuals, continuing to remind them of the concerns and the consequences of the problem should they choose to ignore it.

■ Prospects who have pain, are aware of it and are motivated to seek a solution. These are prospects, but not yet fully qualified, as you have yet to determine their financial capability to solve the problem, as well as their decision-making process. These are individuals who are in the bottom of your pain funnel and have made the decision to work with you if they're convinced you are capable of providing a solution.

Obviously, the individuals in the last two categories provide the best opportunity for business. Concentrate your efforts with these types of prospects, while maintaining contact with the others. Think carefully about how to categorize your potential prospects. Be cautious in your diagnosis regarding their awareness of their problem and their desire to solve it. Although you may want the prospects to be more concerned and motivated about their problem than they are, the prospects determine their motivation to purchase. As you delve more deeply into the personal pains of individuals in these last two groups, while also developing your skills to help the first two groups become aware of their problems, your Business Development efforts will be more successful.

What is Pain? A Closer Look

What exactly do we mean by pain? We can understand the concept more clearly by looking carefully at a few key words that are often misused in the

Business Development Process. From the perspective of Professional Business Development, consider these definitions:

■ Pain – Personal or corporate discomfort being experienced in the absence of the solution.

■ Problem – Physical or intellectual description of an undesirable situation.

■ Interest – Intellectual curiosity to learn what's new and different, to keep up to date.

■ Need – The desired situation or expectation. Where we want to be.

■ Solution – Process or system that will get us to where we want to be.

These terms can be understood more clearly in a real-life example. Take, for instance, a business that provides engineering support services to other consulting engineering firms. Here's how each term might manifest itself:

■ A Problem experienced by the consulting engineering firm would be the inability to solve specific engineering/technical problems on a timely basis. This problem leads to:

■ Corporate Pain of the consulting engineering firm being unable to respond to their customers' requests for services and the potential loss of business... and

■ Personal Pain of individuals with the engineering firm from listening to customers and upper management complaints and the general perception that they are not doing their job.

■ The Need is a method of engineering staff outsourcing so that the consulting engineering firm is able to respond to their customers' requests in a timely manner.

■ A Solution might be a staff augmentation contract to provide a set number of hours of specific engineering services at an agreed price.

■ Interest, in the context of this example, would simply be curiosity about what types of outsource engineering services are available from your company.

What's the point of all this classification of terms? Simply to clarify your own thinking as you consider your prospects' situations.

For example, do not confuse an interest in your product or service with a real need for a solution to a problem. There may not be a problem, or there may be one that the prospect is aware of but may not want to do anything about. You must first be sure to define the problem accurately in the mind of the prospect and have him acknowledge it from his perspective. The ability to get the prospect to acknowledge the problem from his perspective and visualize his need for a solution consistent with the features and benefits of your product or service is critical. Don't start mentally with your product or service as the solution. Dissect the business situations your prospect faces in a way that will help you determine if there is a problem and this will help him become concerned about solving it for his own reasons.

Do not confuse an interest in your product or service with a real need for a solution to a problem.

The Pain Progression
Another helpful concept in understanding your prospect's pain is that of the Pain Progression. This is the sequence of events an individual will connect

together when faced with a problem. Think of it as an internal conversation the troubled prospect has with himself.

Say, for example, I am the engineering manager of a major production firm. My equipment is experiencing a lot of down time and a high reject rate.

What does that say about my ability to maintain production systems?
Nothing good.

What will that lead to?
If it continues, I'll probably receive an unfavorable review.

If the situation gets really bad, what could happen?
I could get fired.

If I get fired, who would hire me as an engineering manager?
No one, perhaps!

If I don't get another job, I'll be out of money. Then what?
I'll starve.

And what does starvation lead to?
Right, death!

Though it's not completely realistic, and even a little funny, the Pain Progression is a subconscious reality in every prospect who has a real and significant pain. It's a clear sequence of events leading from the problem right to a personal threat to the prospect. In reality, several of the intervening points could feel enough like death to move the prospect to a problem-solving decision.

As a Professional in Business Development, you can use your awareness of the Pain Progression to ask questions that might lead the prospect a notch or two through the progression until a solution seems attractive. Again, you cannot make the prospect decide to buy. He or she will buy for their reasons only. But you can use the Pain Progression concept in a subtle way to plant ideas, make suggestions, and otherwise make it convenient for the prospect to see the sequence of painful events that could possibly occur.

Orchestrating Progressive Pain

As you conduct an interview with a prospect, if you are a skilled diagnostician, the prospect will progress through five mental Pain Progression stages.

■ Neutral – The prospect begins at a neutral point. If asked, he or she might say, "I don't have any thoughts one way or another relative to a problem you may be able to help me with."

■ Aware/Interested – Once you begin to ask questions, the person may develop an awareness of a concern or problem. For example, you might ask, "If we were to discuss any concerns you may or may not have about your laboratory operations, what would you want to discuss first?"

The prospective client might respond, "I'm sure, like most hospitals, we're watchful about the productivity of our laboratory technicians."

The client recognizes the subject of laboratory productivity as a topic of importance and is willing to discuss the issue.

■ Concerned – The client's recognition that a concern exists and that it could be harmful warrants further discussion. You discuss the degree of the problem and its implications. As you discuss the potential exposure or dollars at risk, the client decides to conduct a thorough diagnosis of the situation.

- Critical – The critical stage is the point at which the cost of the problem has been defined and has been found to be significant. It is also the point at which the impact or risk of not solving the problem has an ongoing significant impact on people. A critical situation not dealt with for any period of time ultimately leads to a crisis.

- Crisis – The crisis stage is the point at which the pain, problem or lack of action cannot be ignored. It's the point at which the decision-makers recognize that if the situation is not dealt with, they could be cited for incompetence or professional misconduct and place their organization in serious jeopardy.

The successful diagnosis is a blending of the client's knowledge of the symptoms and the situation, and the Business Development Professional's diagnostic and communication skills.

Keep in mind that as a Business Development Professional, you do not create the pain. The pain existed before the diagnostic process began. As a skilled diagnostician, you have simply helped the client become aware of the pain through a systematic communication process. You do not create pain. You help the client discover it and heighten their awareness of it. The successful diagnosis is a blending of the client's knowledge of the symptoms and the situation, and the Business Development Professional's diagnostic and communication skills.

Remedy Versus Disease

An important point that's often overlooked is the undeniable fact that the cure for any pain can be painful itself. Remember we said earlier that "People will not change until the pain of changing is less than the pain they are in." And remember, as a skilled Professional in Business Development, one of your primary roles is managing the pains of your client.

Can you imagine a physician asking a patient to agree to undergo an operation without clearly explaining the potential risks and discomfort the operation will entail? Yet many desperate or deceptive salespeople will not only avoid discussing the pain involved in their solution, but attempt to paint the ensuing picture as a trouble-free sky full of rainbows.

As a skilled Professional in Business Development, one of your primary roles is managing the pains of your client.

What are some of the pains of changing that you should discuss with your client? Here are a few:

■ Dealing with a new company. How easy is it for your clients to do business with your company, and how are you going to make it easier?

■ The pain of paying for the product or service.

■ The pain of changing operating procedures to use the new product or service.

■ Other possible difficulties related to the client's unique situation.

As a Professional in Business Development, be sure you take seriously your responsibility to make your client aware of these potential pains. Your client will encounter these difficulties, whether or not you warn him. Your candor will help him minimize the difficulties, and it will help build the foundation for a solid, long-term business relationship.

Why Prospects Don't Buy

Just when you think you are beginning to understand the reasons people buy, you may be startled to consider that you must also understand why they don't – and shouldn't – buy.

Unlike the traditional "salesperson," who will try to manipulate the sale no matter what, for any reason, to any prospect, the skilled Professional in Business Development is more concerned about the long-term value of his relationship with the client. He knows that in the long run, the best interests of his clients are, in fact, his own best interests. This professional has learned to balance his purpose in Business Development with his goals in Business Development.

No match is better than a forced match between solutions and pain. It is best to under-promise and over-deliver.

That's why the Professional Business Partner is extremely careful in his diagnosis. He knows that people shouldn't buy when the product or service he offers will not improve their business or personal life or provide them with a positive return on their investment. The professional recognizes these situations and knows that a purchase should not occur. Much more valuable in the long run is an honest appraisal of the client's situation. As conditions change, the Professional in Business Development will monitor the relevant factors and initiate the diagnostic process again when a change justifies it. Having been straightforward with the client in this manner, he is likely to be welcomed back.

Your ability to understand the prospect's problem from his perspective early in the diagnostic interview, when he senses that you are more concerned with providing him a solution than with making a sale, is what will earn his trust.

There are three basic reasons why people should not buy from you:

- There is no pain. This implies there is no difference between where they are now and where they want to be in the future.

- There is no match. This happens when you have offered either too little or too much of a solution. Each of us needs to know specifically what solutions we are capable of providing to our clients based on the products or services that we provide. Too often we find ourselves providing solutions to problems that don't exist or trying to convince the prospect we have a solution when in fact it is not the best solution to the specific problem. No match is better than a forced match between solutions and pain. The old adage holds true to this day: It is best to under-promise and over-deliver.

The mark of the true Business Development Professional is a sure and constant focus on the pains of his or her clients.

■ There is no crisis. If there is pain, but the client's pain of change is greater than the pain of staying the same, it is not time in his mind for a solution.

There's one other reason why people don't buy – even when they should. Luckily, it's one that you can control completely. Quite often, people don't buy because there is a lack of trust. In this situation, there is the awareness of pain on the part of the prospect and the desire to relieve the pain. Also, the proposed solution will do the job, but the prospect does not believe the solution will work or believe in the individual providing the solution. Your ability to understand the prospect's problem from his perspective early in the diagnostic interview, when he senses that you are more concerned with providing him a solution than with making a sale, is what will earn his trust. Ultimately there are no degrees of trust. It either exists or it doesn't. Trust is almost always due to the behavior of the professional representing the product. His behavior is a reflection of his principles and beliefs. As a Professional in Business Development, you must operate from a position of confidence, independence, honesty and integrity, ensuring that your prospects are not hampered by this reason not to buy.

Providing Peace of Mind

The mark of the true Business Development Professional is a sure and constant focus on the pains of his or her clients. If you can identify these pains and provide solutions for them, you will undoubtedly be successful. Remember what we said earlier in our discussion of Goals and Purpose? Your Purpose is to help your clients meet their needs, and if you can do this, they will help you meet your Goals of financial success.

In the long view, as a Business Development Professional, you are not merely providing products or services. You are supplying your clients with peace of mind. Your job is to take items off your client's worry list. And to the extent you engage yourself fully in that task, you will find that your business life, your client relationships and your income will bring you peace of mind as well.

In the long view, as a Business Development Professional, you are supplying your clients with peace of mind. Your job is to take items off your client's worry list.

8

Learning The Business Development Process

Now that you've begun to look at the conceptual limitations that must be overcome to succeed and you've learned to understand why people buy,

If you don't have a system or process, you will be part of someone else's – in this case, most likely your prospect's system.

you're ready to begin the "mechanical" part of your education: building a proactive Business Development System. This chapter and the ones that follow will help you develop a specific process for putting into action the principles and concepts you've been learning since Chapter 1. You'll learn to combine these principles and their applied techniques to develop a Business Development System that will work for you, your company, and your client.

Why a System?

Why do you need a system? For several reasons. Remember the concept we discussed earlier: If you don't have a system or process, you will be part of someone else's – in this case, most likely your prospect's system. By your own choice, you will allow your prospect or customer to use you for his or her own agenda. It's far better to be working on your own process to control the outcome of the relationship to both parties' mutual advantage. Fundamentally, a system or a process is a series of proactive steps that bring about a predetermined outcome. Having such a system makes for a lower-risk situation. You will naturally feel more confident making calls and conducting Diagnostic Interviews with prospects. Consequently, you will do more of it. Compare your work as a Professional in Business Development to that of a professional in another fairly risky business – an airline pilot, for example. If you are a trained airline pilot stationed in Boston, you could probably take off in a 767 from Boston on a clear day and, flying along the interstate, visually locate the airport in Philadelphia and land without using any sophisticated instruments. But would you be allowed to do that? Of course not. You would be required to use radar, an altimeter, electronic compass and other instrumentation in the aircraft, plus the computerized air traffic control system and a takeoff and landing checklist. Why? To minimize the risk of harm to yourself and the public.

In just the same way, if you are to function as a Professional in Business Development, you must have a system and use it consciously and proactively. A professional system will:

- Enable you to be better organized and proactive;

- Increase your efficiency and effectiveness;

- Give direction to your Business Development efforts;

- Provide a means for measuring your progress;

- Increase your understanding of why certain techniques work or don't work; and

- Force you to grow professionally and personally.

If you're operating in a Business Development-driven environment, as opposed to a marketing-driven environment, your need for a Business Development System is even greater.

If you are to function as a Professional in Business Development, you must have a system and use it consciously and proactively.

What's the difference? In a marketing-driven environment, the demand for solutions is greater than the supply. The number of prospects who have problems, are aware of them, and want to do something about them is greater than the number of solutions available. This causes sufficient pain and leads prospects to seek a solution. This situation leads to short-term sales that depend on external circumstances. Virtually anyone can sell in this environment. In fact, this type of selling amounts to little more than order-taking. It centers on "features and benefits" marketing and requires little skill. Typical examples are found in the fast food, retail and direct marketing industries, where demand is virtually guaranteed.

In a Business Development-driven environment, prospects don't have a high degree of knowledge regarding your company or your services, what problems you can solve for them, or even if they have any problems.

A Business Development-driven environment, on the other hand, requires much more of the Business Development Professional. Typically, in this environment, prospects don't have a high degree of knowledge regarding your company or your services. They don't know what problems you can solve for them, or even if they have any problems. In this environment, you must be proactive. You must be able to initiate contact by your own effort, find out what the situation is with the suspect or prospect, and act accordingly. Through this process, you must identify the individuals who have problems, are aware of them, and want to do something about them.

Often, when you find a prospect with a problem, you must develop his or her awareness of the problem. You must find those who have interest but no pain and stay in contact with them until they experience sufficient pain to seek a solution. You must study all your prospects, categorize them, and track them. Sooner or later, they drop through your "Pain Funnel" to become qualified prospects – or you remove them from the funnel and add someone else in their place.

The difference in developing business in a Business Development-driven, versus a marketing-driven, environment is the difference between being proactive and being reactive.

As you can readily see, the difference in developing business in a Business Development-driven, versus a marketing-driven, environment is the difference between being proactive and being reactive. It's the difference between an independent approach and a dependent approach that relies on external market conditions.

Chances are you find yourself operating in a Business Development-driven environment or you would not likely be a candidate for this level of training. The more Business Development-driven you are, the more you require a proactive process. It is important to remember we are not talking about a reactive traditional selling system. What we are discussing here is a proactive system for prospecting, qualifying and tracking leads. This type of system is far more efficient than a "selling system." The top three percent of Business Development people, the Professional Business Partners we've been discussing, are master prospectors and qualifiers. One of their unique characteristics is that they know how to efficiently and effectively disqualify individuals early. They know exactly what problems they can solve for clients, they know what these problems look like, and they can quickly determine if the

The top three percent of Business Development people, the Professional Business Partners we've been discussing, are master prospectors and qualifiers.

prospect has them. Their radar is constantly working to detect the presence of significant problems among their prospects and clients.

Components of a Successful Business Development System

Now let's get down to brass tacks and look at the development of a Seven-Step system for professionally turning prospects into customers.

As you begin to implement any system or process, it is important to understand that it must be part of your Goals and plans and be complemented with skills that you can use with your style or personality. Every contact you make with a suspect or prospect should be evaluated against what your Goals were for that contact and how you are going to achieve them with your plan. At the conclusion of the contact, you should be able to determine where you are in your Business Development Process and what skills you utilized to move the prospect forward in the process. Your Business Development System and related skills must be part of your short-term and long-term Goals and plans to be a successful Professional in the role of Business Development.

Your Business Development System and related skills must be part of your short-term and long-term Goals and plans to be a successful Professional in the role of Business Development.

In our workshops, we often ask our participants to define the characteristics they believe are important in a professional, proactive Business Development System – one that they would design and have confidence in using. Typical characteristics they look for include a system or process that is easy to understand and execute and one that is win/win for all parties involved. They also mention that such a system needs to be efficient and effective, one that saves time for themselves and their prospect, allowing each party to share the most information in the shortest amount of time. They want a system that includes no pressure for either party and does not require the Business Development Professional to sell or push any solution or product.

They also mention the need to have a process that works both short-term in developing business and in maintaining a long-term, positive relationship. Ultimately, they define a system that is professional and, that would reflect the thinking of a business person, not a traditional salesperson.

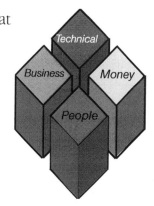

An analogy that we have often used to describe such a system and that is part of the corporate trademark of MBD[i] is the space shuttle. Just as in the launch of NASA's space shuttle, many

THE 4 CORNERSTONES OF BUSINESS DEVELOPMENT

steps and complex processes are completed before the final countdown is reached and the shuttle is successfully launched. To oversimplify that process, some of the steps would include preplanning, the definition of the mission objectives, the training and preparation of the flight crew and other mission coordinators, a pre-launch check process, shuttle launch, mission execution and, ultimately, re-entry and return.

We relate these steps to seven critical steps that are important for the Business Development Professional to execute before considering any significant presentation of his or her product or service to a prospect. Those seven steps are:

1. Homework Before the Call
Before you make your initial contact with your suspect or prospect, it is essential that you do your homework. This homework is centered around the Four Cornerstones of Business Development: business information, money information, people information and technical information. It includes gathering information on your prospect's company, their problem, personal information on your prospect and other related information to help you understand the prospect's world from his or her perspective. It is

important to review this information prior to every call, but it is critical before the first. Most initial calls are made with some degree of technical information, but vastly lacking in the other three. There is much you need to know about your prospect. What is his or her area of responsibility? To whom does he or she report? Who are his or her subordinates? What are his or her Goals within the organization? What is his or her political position within the company? Likewise, extensive information needs to be gathered, analyzed and understood regarding the operation of the company and how they make money.

You will be positioned in relation to the prospect and treated by the prospect consistent with your level of thinking.

2. Bonding and Positioning

The bonding process is the foundation for building a symbiotic relationship between you and your prospect. This step should establish trust, honesty, and respect and form the basis of a mutually satisfactory business relationship. This is the first part of the Business Development Process that forms the marriage, aimed at ensuring that both parties are working from a win/win position. Bonding is basically the process of being seen by the prospects as similar to themselves. The second part of this step is the positioning process. You will be positioned in relation to the prospect and treated by the prospect consistent with your level of thinking. It is critical in this step that you position yourself as a business person in relation to the prospect rather than as a salesperson. Your credibility in establishing this position will be judged by the level and type of questions you ask, not the statements you make.

3. Communicating Goal and Purpose of the Relationship and Negotiating the Rules Rights and Responsibilities in the Relationship

In this step of the Business Development System you establish the rights of each party in the relationship, as well as the Purpose, Goals, Responsibilities and Rules of the symbiotic association between you and your prospect. This enables each of you to know the parameters of what is intended to be a Professional Business Development relationship. Covering this step early with your prospect positions you as a professional and lets the prospect know you intend to proceed only if you can establish a mutually beneficial professional relationship.

Your credibility in establishing this position will be judged by the level and type of questions you ask, not the statements you make.

4. Obtaining Permission to Interview for Problems
Prior to beginning a Diagnostic Interview to uncover pain, you must gain permission to proceed to this level. A level of trust and respect must be established prior to this step and the Rules of the Relationship must be clearly understood. Prior to beginning the process of qualifying the prospect based on his problems, permission must be received in order for him to be up-front in giving you the information you will require.

5. The Diagnostic Interview
In this step you will begin a process of asking the prospect specific questions regarding concerns, problems or pains he may or may not have. It is in this step that you qualify or disqualify the prospect based on his reason for needing to purchase. By understanding how and why the prospect buys, you are able in this step to help him recognize and take ownership of problems he hasn't been aware of and become motivated to address them with your products or services.

6. Determining the Prospect's Financial Commitment to Address his Concerns
In this step all of the costs of the solution are discussed, and an evaluation is made of the prospect's willingness to make the financial investment necessary to secure a solution to the identified problems. It is at this point that the prospect is able to relate intellectually the cost associated with the solution to the problems identified and acknowledged as needing attention.

7. Determining the Decision-Making Process

During this step, you will identify Who makes the appropriate decisions and When and How those decisions are made. All three factors are critical prior to a presentation, and it is necessary for the prospect to be in a position to make whatever decision is appropriate at the designated time. All decision-makers will be identified during this step of the process, and a detailed understanding will be established as to when and how a decision will be made.

Several additional characteristics of this System are important to understand. First, it allows the prospect to self-qualify and always allows him the opportunity to say "no." This assures both parties a relationship where there is no pressure on either side, and one which encourages honest communication by everyone toward meeting mutual objectives. Second, it allows any information gathered at any time to be appropriately evaluated and processed during any step. Third, it allows you to proceed with the System and process as far as you are comfortable and capable at any time and to re-engage with the prospect at any future time, covering any information necessary to proceed. Fourth, it is a System that can be used by multiple individuals within your organization to coordinate the development of a multifaceted account that requires the development of relationships with multiple individuals. In this and additional chapters, we will cover each of these steps in detail, providing for your understanding of both the process necessary to execute the techniques and the thinking necessary to be perceived in the position as a Professional in Business Development.

The Importance of the First Three Steps

These first three steps are critical to the successful execution of this Business Development System. The thinking that you develop in doing your homework and the manner in which you Position and Bond with the prospect, as well as the way you communicate your Purpose and Goal and establish the Rules Rights and Responsibilities of the Relationship, form the basis on which you will be seen and treated as a Professional Business Partner, the top 3 percent of performers in sales and Business Development. How you execute these first three steps is a direct reflection of your level of thinking. It is important that we approach these three steps from the mental perspective of a professional business person looking to develop a long-term,

mutually beneficial business relationship with the prospect or client. The mental perspective of approaching the prospect with a long-term view will generate more business for you directly and indirectly than approaching from a short-term perspective, looking for the quick sale. Each of these steps takes time to plan and execute, but is time well-invested. Your ability to execute these three steps on a professional level allows you to disqualify certain prospects for business reasons and allows you to quickly move to other prospects to qualify or disqualify based on their specific pain. The old axioms that a job well begun is half done, and that good matters get better and bad matters get worse, hold true in the execution of this Professional Business Development process.

Step 1: Homework Before the Call

Three critical items must be considered in your Homework Before the Call. First, what information do you have or do you need to determine before initiating this call, based on the Four Cornerstones of Business Development? The information you've gathered will be categorized in four critical areas: business knowledge, money knowledge, people knowledge and technical knowledge. Second, prior to initiating any contact with the prospect, either an initial contact or a follow-up, it is important that you ask yourself more questions. First, what is my specific Goal on this call? Second, what is my plan for attaining this Goal? Third, at what step of my Business

Development System am I starting, and fourth, what skills or techniques will be necessary to advance the prospect with this system? Your Homework Before the Call is one of the least commonly used yet most critical steps. Prior to any call, you must gather all the information you can regarding the business you are going to call on, its people, how they make money, and appropriate technical information about their product or service and the problems you will solve.

The mental perspective of approaching the prospect with a long-term view will generate more business for you directly and indirectly than approaching from a short-term perspective, looking for the quick sale.

From a business perspective, you should know everything about your prospect's product or service, market and customers, and their structure and organization. You must understand how they make money. How do they turn their products and services into profit? Find out everything you can about the organization. Who is in charge of what areas? Why? Find out areas of responsibility, authority and influence. Technically, what problem can you solve for them, and why is it critical that the problem be solved? The information you gather before the call, initial or follow-up, lays the foundation for Step Two. This information can be gathered from a variety of sources: prior contacts, business contacts, business news, Dun and Bradstreet, the Internet and a multitude of other places. You will use this information in your next step in formulating questions to Bond and Position with the prospect, so it is important that the homework you do be organized and complete.

Step 2: Bonding and Positioning
This step sets the tone for the total business relationship. The ability to meet with or call on a prospect or customer and develop a one-on-one business relationship is invaluable. Bonding is the process of externally positioning yourself from the prospects' perspective, moving into their world and seeing their situation from their perspective. Prior to this step, you have already

gathered information about their company, products, market, people, business and method of making money. This information affords you the opportunity to move into their world and be seen as an individual who is sincerely interested in their situation. The ability to ask them questions regarding what you have already determined in your Homework allows you to be seen as one of them, seeing their world from their perspective. Bonding is the process of asking the questions about what is interesting, important and relevant to them, not you. For many of the questions you ask, you may

The type and level of questions you ask in the Bonding process allow you to be positioned with the prospect or customer as a Professional in Business Development.

already know the answer. Regardless, they will understand these questions and will value being asked. The type and level of questions you ask in the Bonding process allow you to be positioned with the prospect or customer as a Professional in Business Development. The Homework you have done before the call will help you immeasurably in portraying the image of a business person seeking to ask the appropriate questions. The prospect will see you as a professional seeking a long-term business relationship rather than a salesperson trying to make a short-term sale.

Step 3: Communicating the Purpose and Goal of the Relationship and Negotiating the Rules Rights and Responsibilities of that Relationship
Discuss early with your prospect what you want to accomplish by working together. Concentrate on establishing the basic structure of your relationship. Express to him that you are a business person assisting him in solving business, people, money or technical problems by providing a product or service for a fee. Your ability to communicate to the prospect early your Purpose as well as your Goal will ensure that you are received as a business person. Relate to your prospect that your Purpose is to help him figure out what problems he may have and what solutions are available, as well as your Goal of determining if he is a valid prospect for your company's services.

How might you do this? Here's an example: Tell the client you'd like to talk to him about his expectations. Ask him to share those expectations and tell him you'd like to share with him the way you typically begin your relationship with a prospect or client.

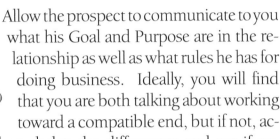

Allow the prospect to communicate to you what his Goal and Purpose are in the relationship as well as what rules he has for doing business. Ideally, you will find that you are both talking about working toward a compatible end, but if not, acknowledge the differences and see if appropriate middle ground can be agreed upon. Introduce your intentions in a straightforward, up-front conversation. Also, during this conversation, negotiate early the Rules, Rights and Responsibilities of each party in the Relationship. In any business relationship, you both have certain rights as professionals. You must know what rights you have and be able to communicate them in a professional manner: the right to be treated as a professional, the right to appropriate information, the right to ask questions and give information. Remember this rule: You have rights, but you also have responsibilities. Your prospect also has rights, and you must be sure that both of you agree on the rules of the relationship and the rights and expectations each individual has. Discuss with your prospect his expectations regarding your relationship. Then share with him your customary way of beginning a new relationship with a client. Doing so establishes a professional tone for your relationship. This one simple step will identify you to the prospect as a professional, not an amateur – as a business person, not a salesperson. Business professionals establish rules of the relationship up-front. Sales-

Remember this rule: You have rights, but you also have responsibilities.

people are focused on making short-term sales. Individuals with traditional sales thinking have not addressed the principles that guide their behavior, identified their mission, nor clearly understand their Purpose. Therefore, they struggle with this level of conversation. They are still focused on the thought, "How do I get this sale? What do I have to do?" You must let the prospect know you are not interested in simply selling him something and then moving on. Instead, you want to solve his problems and in the process make a profit for yourself and your company.

These first three steps of our Seven-Step Business Development Process set the tone for the whole process and determine at what level you will be working with the prospect or client.

Throughout these first three steps, your Purpose is to help the prospect discover what problems he or she has and how to solve them. Your Goal is to determine if he or she is a viable prospect for your company. These first three steps of our Seven-Step Business Development Process set the tone for the whole process and determine at what level you will be working with the prospect or client. Correctly executing these three steps puts you in the top 3 percent of professionals in Business Development. Getting used to this approach is not easy. It takes time to master, but is more than worth the effort because it sets a Professional tone for your entire relationship with your prospect.

Evaluating Your First Three Steps

Before you move forward to the Diagnostic Interview, you should conduct a thorough evaluation of your first three steps. Much as NASA does a preflight check before moving forward on the shuttle launch, this is an evaluation of how strong a link has been developed between you and your prospect that will form a basis for a mutually satisfying partnership as a potential deal develops.

Your ability to Bond and Position and establish the rules of the relationship develops a high degree of trust, respect, and honesty up-front, ensuring that both you and your prospect are working on a win/ win basis. Your Goal in these first three steps is that the prospect sees and treats you as a professional, feels you are in tune with him or her and is completely comfortable with you.

People do business with people. The more you understand the individual and the more he relates to you as a person, the more he will want to do business with you.

Fundamental to these steps is knowing your prospect as an individual. During these steps, spend as much time as possible focusing on the individual you are dealing with. Find out everything you can about how he thinks, what he believes, and what his motivation is in the relationship. People do business with people. The more you understand the individual and the more he relates to you as a person, the more he will want to do business with you.

These initial steps of our Business Development process involve the exchange of intellectual transactions. In terms of the Parent, Adult, Child framework we discussed in earlier chapters, these will be transactions between your Adult and the prospect's Adult. You will talk about his business, where he is and how he got there, what he does and how he does it. As long as you are collecting data on the business, the client will remain in the Adult mode. As you move forward and begin to talk about the problems in his business, you may move more into the area of the Child.

Remember this rule: No telling, no selling. If you approach a prospecting call in an internally focused way, simply trying to sell something and get your needs met, you will fail.

By proactively taking control of the situation up-front, you will convey to your prospect that you have a process and a system. You want to be sure you are not doing either of two things. Remember this rule: No telling, no selling. This is absolutely critical during your initial contacts. If you approach a prospecting call in an internally focused way, simply trying to sell something and get your needs met, you will fail. The prospect will sense what you are doing and instinctively will not trust you.

Critical to your successful execution of the first three steps of your system is your understanding of the difference between the Purpose of Business Development and the Goal of Business Development. The Purpose of Business Development is external – what you can and will do for your client. The Goal of Business Development is internal – what you are doing for yourself. You are the president of You, Inc., and as such you have your own Goals for your career in Business Development. You can meet these Goals by fulfilling the Purpose of Business Development, which is solving problems for your client. If you cannot honestly convey to your prospects that your Purpose is to help them recognize, become aware of and deal with their problems, they will see you as an individual interested only in yourself, rather than them. You must understand there is a difference between your Purpose and your Goal, and that you must always put your Purpose, the needs of your prospect or client, ahead of your own. Remember, if your Purpose is to help your prospect or client get his needs met, he will help you reach your Goals.

Conceptual Limitations to Executing Steps 2 and 3

In both yourself and your prospect, there may exist psychological factors that inhibit the Bonding process. Again, we are talking about the psychological baggage you bring to your role in Business Development, the "six inches between your ears." And what may be even more difficult to understand is the psychological baggage that your prospect brings to the transaction as well.

As we discussed in Chapter 6, one of the most critical tools for success in Business Development is a basic understanding of human psychology. As

133

you come to understand your own "life position" based on conditioning from your early experiences, you will also no doubt gain insights that help you understand the life positions of your clients.

Your first task is to manage your own emotional baggage. Make sure your half of any business transaction is not hampered by Not OK feelings within yourself. Of course, it will take a lifetime to master this skill completely. Nevertheless, by continually measuring and evaluating your feelings and actions, by reminding yourself that your role-identity and your self-identity are distinctly separate, you can keep yourself feeling relatively OK in transactions with any prospect.

Your next task, then, is to evaluate the prospect's behavior and seek to understand what sort of life position he or she is coming from. Does the prospect act as though she feels Not OK? As you discuss her problems and the solutions you offer, does she need to put you down in order to feel OK herself?

Remember that being a prospect can be, in itself, a Not OK situation. The prospect may feel she doesn't know enough about her work to carry it out correctly. Especially if she is having significant problems, she may feel inadequate in the face of these challenges. This feeling can unearth long-held self-concepts of unworthiness and low self-esteem. In addition, she has to spend money to solve her problem, a prospect she does not relish. She has an uncertain situation on her hands. She is not sure if your product can solve her problem, and she is wary of gambling away her company's money on something that may not work.

Few if any prospects will buy from a Business Development person to whom they feel inferior.

By the time you arrive in her office, your prospect may already feel like the six-year-old who has just spilled her milk all over the dining room table. If you appear to know a great deal more than your prospect about her work operation or try to dazzle her with details that show your mastery of the subject, you may contribute to her feelings of ignorance and unworthiness.

It is far better to ask questions, show empathy and gently lead the prospect to your solution than to breeze in as God's gift to industry, the know-it-all who has come to save this poor benighted business from an early death. If you appear on the doorstep obviously feeling 200 percent OK and your prospect has a bad case of the Not OKs, you are likely to elicit an icy reception and a polite "we'll call you" from your unhappy prospect. You will lose the sale, and the prospect will lose the real benefit she might have derived from your product.

Few if any prospects will buy from a Business Development person to whom they feel inferior. Resist the temptation to show how much you know and, in the process, alienate your prospect so that all opportunity for bonding is destroyed.

It is your responsibility to manage the Not OK feelings that can be aroused by the dynamics of any Business Development transaction.

On the other hand, you are not likely to complete a favorable business transaction with a prospect to whom YOU feel inferior. If your prospect is feeling OK and you are in the "please love me-buy my product" mode, she will naturally mistrust you. While she will not be comfortable if you are arrogant, neither will she be comfortable if you are meek and uncertain. She needs to trust your abilities and your product in order to buy from you. If you are operating from the I'm Not OK-You're OK position, your prospect will react negatively, making you feel even more Not OK and dashing all hope of a positive outcome. Thus it is your responsibility to manage the Not

OK feelings that can be aroused by the dynamics of any Business Development transaction.

You can do this by careful and continuing self-examination that aims at rooting out all vestiges of unjustified Not OK feelings planted during your past. As we have discussed, this is a lifelong task, one that is probably never completely finished. But your diligence and success in this area will be clearly indicated by your success in Business Development. You will find an immediate and direct correlation between your own emotional health and your Business Development success.

Many Business Development people, because of the Not OK feelings they bring to their role, allow themselves to call on prospects who are not at the proper decision-making level.

A particular caution in this regard: Many Business Development people, because of the Not OK feelings they bring to their role, allow themselves to call on prospects who are not at the proper decision-making level. They find it easier to imagine the Bonding process taking place between themselves and a junior representative of the prospect company than, say, the CEO or the vice president. In actuality, this is a false perception. Most people don't care about your title. If you can speak their language, on their level of business expertise, they will easily and happily bond with you.

Don't allow your own lingering feelings of inferiority – which can easily be aroused by the challenges of the Business Development relationship – trick you into this cop-out. Do you rationalize a more comfortable prospecting situation by deciding you might offend the person who holds the higher position? Whatever you may tell yourself is only a subterfuge for your own fear and insecurity.

Summon your courage, tell yourself that you are the president of You, Inc., pick up the phone and call the president – or whoever is truly appropriate.

Remember: It is always easier to come down the hill than it is to go up. You will be more successful starting at the top. This way you avoid an uncertain struggle to find out later who is actually in control, who can decide to buy your product.

Remember, too, that because Bonding must take place before your prospect will buy, you must do all you can to ensure the two of you develop an "I'm OK-You're OK" relationship. By negotiating up-front the Rules and Rights of your business Relationship, you set the stage for this win-win position. By waiting until every detail is ready for launching, you reinforce this professional stance. And by listening attentively and exhibiting empathy, not arrogance or inferiority, you facilitate the necessary Bonding that can lead to mutual business success.

Most people don't care about your title. If you can speak their language, on their level of business expertise, they will easily and happily bond with you.

9

The Diagnostic Process:
Steps 4 and 5

By now you've determined the importance of the first three steps of your Business Development process. During steps 2 and 3 of Bonding, Positioning, covering Rules Rights and Responsibilities and Goal and Purpose, you've been sharing primarily intellectual information. Now it is time to add emotional information, the basic ingredient for establishing pain in the prospect. This information is acquired through the interviewing process. You will need both types of information. The intellectual information from the Adult Ego State allows you to gather data about the prospect. This data will help you put together a picture of the potential client and his or her company. It will fill in important facts and figures about the business and potential areas in which your product or service may be helpful. During the first three steps of the system, based on the information you've received, you can evaluate whether you have a potential prospect or simply a suspect. You can determine whether the person you're speaking with matches your profile of a typical prospect. Keep in mind that the intellectual information that you gather early in your conversations is not in itself a revelation of pain, but merely information about the organization and the individual.

The essential emotional information you'll need will come from answers to questions of a more personal and emotional nature. These questions are intended to determine first-person personal pain. In this phase of your interview, you'll avoid intellectual questions and approach your prospect from a more personal and emotional standpoint. You'll inquire about fears, frustrations, dislikes, concerns and feelings. This enables the prospect to demonstrate pain, if any, from an emotional point of view and reveals areas of concern from his or her perspective. You'll need to learn how to ask questions like, "What are your major concerns in the area of...? What are your biggest fears regarding...? What is the major frustration when...? What do you dislike most about...?" Your questions in this part of your Business Development process will have emotional words in them. This tone invites your prospect to reply on an emotional level, where the pain, if any, will reside.

You'll need to learn how to ask questions like, "What are your major concerns in the area of...? What are your biggest fears regarding...?"

Before you approach your prospect from this more personal position, you must ask permission to ask these emotionally based questions. We'll talk more about that later. For now, remember that both the intellectual and emotional information you will gather during your interview are equally important. Both are essential if you are to form a realistic evaluation of your prospect and the likelihood of forming a mutually beneficial relationship.

Diagnostic Medicine: An Analogy

Professional Business Development is much like diagnostic medicine. To understand further how your Business Development System can be effective, consider this analogy of how a physical works:

Say, for example, you go to a heart surgeon. He asks, "Where does it hurt?"

You say, "It's my heart, doctor. That's all you need to know. Tell me what the surgery is going to cost, and I'll decide whether or not to do it."

The surgeon might respond, "Well, I have to find out what's causing your pain before I can put together a plan for an operation or treatment. I'll need to ask you a number of questions and run some tests before I can determine the extent of the problem. Then I can give you an idea of how much it will cost."

If you encounter a prospect who is unwilling to invest in the time you need to diagnose the problems of his business, you are probably not losing a likely prospect, but simply ruling out a non-qualified one at an early stage.

You say, "I really don't want to go to all that trouble. Forget it." That implies you don't have enough pain to warrant the pain of the examination. In all probability, you don't have a serious heart problem. Similarly, if you encounter a prospect who is unwilling to invest in the time you need to diagnose the problems of his business, don't despair. You are probably not losing a likely prospect, but simply ruling out a non-qualified one at an early stage. Rejoice and move on to the next one.

The Pain Funnel: The Qualifying Process

Like the physician, your duty as a Professional in Business Development is to locate, diagnose and relieve pain. To be successful in this profession, you must do what we call "keeping your pain funnel full."

This means that, at any time, you have a funnel full of prospects who may have problems you can solve. They will be at different levels in the funnel, based on the progress of your relationship with them. Using your Seven-Step Business Development System, you can determine at which time to move them in your system based on their pain level.

Generally, you will find that there are four categories of suspects/prospects. An effective way to separate them is to understand the "Hierarchy of Pain."

All suspects/prospects are placed in the funnel. Some will go to the top of the funnel, while others work their way to the bottom and end up as legitimate prospects or even customers. What determines their position in the funnel is their level of pain and their desire to alleviate it.

THE PAIN FUNNEL

Some will evaporate along the way because they either don't have a problem, or are not willing to solve it. The only way you can ensure a profitable business for yourself is to keep your funnel full by adding new suspects/prospects to replace those who have departed. Along the way you will identify four levels of suspects or prospects.

▪ Level 1 Suspect – This person will have an intellectual interest in your products or services but no visible pain for you to explore or resolve. A high level of intellectual interest, without a corresponding pain, will be an indicator that the suspect hasn't enough money to justify addressing the problem. Don't waste a lot of time with suspects like these. You will be interested that they are so interested, but in the end you will accomplish little. If you have positively placed someone in this category, it is time to move on and allow this suspect to relinquish his or her space in the funnel to someone else. Your mission is to prospect and qualify, not to educate.

You will find that there are four categories of suspects/ prospects. An effective way to separate them is to understand the "Hierarchy of Pain."

▪ Level 2 Suspect – This is the prospect who has a problem, but is not aware of it. For now, he does not have enough pain emanating from the problem to make him seek a solution. Your response will be to develop the problem's consequences in the client's mind until it begins to cause him pain. Ask questions, probe, and suggest possible ways the problem might grow until the client begins to feel uneasy – until the suspect becomes a prospect. This is best done gently and offhandedly, with low-key statements beginning, "I guess that means you'd never..." or "That probably wouldn't mean you'd later..." or "I don't suppose it could...". Don't paint a dramatic problem that grows into a real tragedy. You'll be met with strong and instantaneous resistance. Simply plant the seeds of uncertainty and get the client thinking about a problem that could grow into a bona fide pain. Then go on to another prospect, checking back periodically to see if your seeds are growing.

Your mission is to prospect and qualify, not to educate.

How can you determine the degree of pain caused by your client's problem? The usual clues include facial expression, body language, and agitation. If your client is stalking around the office while he tells you of his problems, take heart. If not, it will be up to you to develop those areas of potential pain that emerge from your interviews.

Some people feel uncomfortable seeing other individuals in pain and find it difficult to "pick at" painful spots when they see them. Likewise, some people are afraid that once they get an individual in pain, he will turn on them and blame them for it. Strategically developing the client's pain is a delicate art that requires intuition and practice. You can never be too skillful. But with experience, you can learn to develop your prospects' pain until you make them aware of it and get them to take ownership of it. Indeed, you must learn this skill if you are to be successful in Professional Business Development.

Strategically developing the client's pain is a delicate art that requires intuition and practice. You can never be too skillful.

- Level 3 Prospect – This is the prospect who has a problem, knows it, but at this particular time does not want to do anything about it. This is a delicate type of client who requires a lot of gentle picking at the pain, challenging him to take responsibility for it, lest he suffer the consequences. Typically, an individual takes this approach for one of two reasons. He may not want to do anything about it now because he has other problems of a higher priority that need to be addressed at this particular time. It's not that he doesn't want to do anything about it. It's just that he may not be able to do anything about it right now. The skill you need here is to move the problem from the prospect's low priority to a high priority. You can do this by keeping the prospect continually aware of the problem and the ramifications of not solving it.

Secondly, he may not feel ownership of the problem if it does not directly impact him. He has a problem and is aware of it, but solving the problem would not personally affect him. Generally, if the pain is "first-person personal," the suspect/prospect is more motivated to seek a solution.

Often, prospects of this type will try to avoid responsibility for the problem, hoping it will go away. You must gather information about the client's level of responsibility and his desire to address the problem. One of the skills we will cover later in this study is that of "reversing," or discounting the problem with the client and agreeing with him that it will probably never become serious. This will typically provoke a more positive response and a quicker ownership of the situation.

- Level 4 Prospect – This is an individual who has problems, is aware of them, is willing to take ownership of them, and desires a solution. At this point we do not have a fully qualified prospect, because we do not know the investment potential he has available to address the problem, nor do we know completely who would be involved in the decision-making process or when and how they would make a decision. Your challenge here is to be certain that solutions you have available can truly alleviate this individual's pain, and that the prospect believes that you understand his problem from his perspective. A prospect at this level will seek a solution to his problem, but at this point there still remains work to be done. Transforming leads from suspects into prospects requires time, energy, and organization through a system and skills. It requires constant calling and visiting, continually asking questions to raise uncertainties, and allowing time for the prospect to develop his own thinking and concerns regarding his situation. You will very seldom encounter a Level 4 Prospect on your first or second visit. This is why it is essential that you keep your funnel full with multiple individuals to contact. You should keep in contact with your suspect or prospect until it becomes apparent he will never have or recognize his pain. An abundance of prospects will keep you from feeling desperate and applying pressure to rush your prospects into a sale. Keeping your funnel full will allow you to pursue selectively the prospects for whom you can truly solve problems. That means, of course, that you are more likely to form lasting, long-term, profitable Business Development relationships.

Steps 4 and 5 of the Business Development Process

Step 4: Asking Permission to Interview for Pains
You should never proceed into a pain or problem interview without getting permission from the prospect or client up-front. Why? Because of a basic rule: No one can get mad at you for doing what he has given you permission to do. At this step in the system, you are going beyond the superficial information-gathering process and asking permission to ask about first-person personal pains and problems that will ultimately need resolution. This is a step that must be moved into cautiously and with the prospect's

permission. Here are a couple of examples of how to start in this direction: "Would you feel uncomfortable if I asked you about concerns you may or may not have in a specific area?" Or "Would it be appropriate that I ask some questions about concerns or difficulties that may have been encountered in a specific area?"

MBD *insights*

No one can get mad at you for doing what he has given you permission to do.

Step 5: Interviewing the Prospect for Problems and Pain
Remember this rule: Don't ask anyone a question that you didn't ask if you could ask him.

First, you must ask the prospect's permission to ask him a few questions. Always give him permission to say no. It's inherent in his rights in the relationship. At this point, you must have a list of specific problem areas in which there is a reasonable probability the prospect may have difficulties. If you've done your homework ahead of time and worked with other similar prospects or clients, you have an idea of how to begin a Diagnostic Interview to ascertain potential problem areas. Your pain questions must be succinct, direct and effective in helping the prospect discover problems. Determine if the prospect has problems or pains that you have the capacity to solve. Find out if he's aware of them and if he wants to do something about them. Remember that it is more effective to ask negative questions than positive ones. For example, "It is unlikely you've ever encountered..." or "I doubt that you've ever had a problem such as this...". Negative questions are more likely to elicit a more comfortable, positive response.

Your pain questions must be succinct, direct and effective in helping the prospect discover problems.

The Diagnostic Interviewing process may take two hours or two years. For you to be successful there must be pain, an awareness of it on the part of the prospect and motivation on his part to seek a solution. If one or more of these factors aren't present, see if you can develop them in the prospect. If not, remember: It's OK if the prospect says no. Simply put him back into your "funnel" and be on the lookout for possible future pain he may have mentioned. As that pain nears, remember to follow up with the prospect.

Remember: It's OK if the prospect says no.

The Diagnostic Process: Developing Pain

The goal of your Diagnostic Interview in Step 5 is to get your prospect to share with you what his pain looks like, what it feels like to him personally, and how it affects him directly. You need to ask questions that will allow the prospect to describe the problem from his perspective in a way that you can understand.

MBD *insights*

There are only two possible reasons your prospect does not develop into a client: Either there is no pain or you are not skillful enough in uncovering it.

As you have mastered the first three steps of this Business Development System and gone on to Step 4, Asking Permission to Interview for Pain, keep in mind that Step 5, Interviewing the Prospect for Problems and Pain, can be done effectively face-to-face or by telephone. Resist the temptation to delve immediately into a pain interview without first having established the first three steps of your Business Development System in earlier calls.

There are several reasons for following this rule. First, it is more cost-effective. In the days of cell phones, fax machines, e-mail and other electronic communication, you can become much more efficient in sharing information. Do as much of your initial prospecting and qualifying as possible by phone to assure that you will only be investing your face-to-face time on bona fide prospects, not whiling away that time with unqualified "suspects."

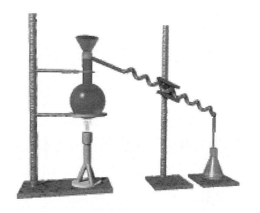

THE PAIN DISTILLATION PROCESS

Another reason is that by conducting as much of your interview as possible by phone, you can use a written script to help you target your questions and keep yourself and the prospect on track. Remember, you want your prospects to be investing as much into this relationship as you are. You want them to desire a solution to their problems. It's often a good idea to give your prospects little tasks to do and see if they are investing in the relationship. Test them using your system. If they won't take a little step they've agreed to do by a certain date, it is a sign they're not really serious about solving their problem. It's better for you to find this out early before you've invested a great deal of your time.

A good test on your initial phone interview or follow-up pain interview is to request that prospects send you some literature or information on their company or problems. Tell them when you receive it, you'll review it and get back to them on additional questions that the two of you need to discuss

The goal of your Diagnostic Interview in Step 5 is to get your prospect to share with you what his pain looks like, what it feels like to him personally, and how it affects him directly.

together. See if they will take this small step. If so, they're committing to you as a prospect. If not, talk to them to find out why, then reevaluate the investment of your time before proceeding.

To be successful in your Diagnostic Interviewing, you must know what to look for. In your search for pain, stay aware of the signals of emotionally based, rather than intellectually based, statements. If a prospect tells you the greatest challenge in his industry is achieving on-time shipments, recognize that he's making an intellectual statement. If he says, "It's driving me nuts. We're working three shifts already, and we just can't get the orders shipped on time!" he's sharing genuine pain. Ask yourself whether your product or service can help alleviate that pain. Unless there's a good match between the specific problem and your service, don't proceed. Be fully aware of what problems you can and cannot solve, and only seek to solve those for which your product or service is effective. Remember: The world is full of potential clients. Invest your time on those that have the greatest likelihood of your being able to help them solve their problems.

You want your prospects to be investing as much into this relationship as you are.

Remember: The world is full of potential clients. Invest your time on those that have the greatest likelihood of your being able to help them solve their problems.

Understanding Why People Buy vs. Selling

As we discussed earlier, there is a key difference between a marketing-driven environment and a Business Development-driven environment. In a marketing-driven environment, the demand for solutions exceeds the supply. Selling is a reactive process – often a matter of making intellectual presentations of "features and benefits" to prospects who already want to buy a product. Virtually anyone can "sell" in this environment.

By definition of your position as a Professional in Business Development, you are likely operating in a Business Development-driven environment, where your solutions are not readily acknowledged by the prospect and the demand for those solutions is unknown. Your challenge is far greater than simply presenting product features and benefits and waiting for the client to sign on the dotted line. You must develop qualified prospects. You must

be able to locate prospects who have problems, work with them until they are keenly
aware of these problems, and continue to
track them until they decide they want to
solve these problems. Yours is a proactive
process. Instead of simply knowing how
to present features and benefits, you must
understand why people would be motivated to purchase your products. Once

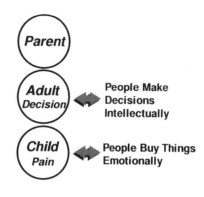

you understand that people buy to alleviate a recognized, emotionally based
pain they are experiencing, you must understand and practice the technique of helping your prospects identify that pain and cure it.

Psychological Dependence vs. Independence

People who need approval are working from a psychologically dependent
position. Those for whom approval is a pleasant added bonus, but not a
psychological necessity, are working from a psychologically independent position.

Having an independent prospecting and qualifying system is the key to being psychologically independent in Business Development. Without the
mind-set and process of proactive Business Development, many people find themselves dependent

*Instead of simply knowing
how to present features and
benefits, you must understand
why people would be motivated
to purchase your products.*

on the limited number of prospects with whom they come in contact. They
tend to overreact, doing whatever they believe necessary to make a short-
term sale. The prospect inevitably senses this and reacts negatively.

Professionals who understand how and why people buy, and who understand the balance between their purpose and their goal in Business Development, realize that there is an abundance of opportunities in the marketplace to develop business. Their challenge is how to efficiently qualify or

disqualify suspects/prospects. Psychologically independent Professionals in Business Development have a solid prospecting, qualifying and lead-tracking system that they know they can rely on. They use this system to structure their behavior, and they understand the value of disqualifying suspects early. They understand that getting "no's" early is not failure. They are focused on finding the qualified prospect who is willing to buy for his or her own reasons, and they realize that they do not have to make the sale.

Having an independent prospecting and qualifying system is the key to being psychologically independent in Business Development.

With careful thought and disciplined practice, you can move yourself from a psychologically dependent "sales" position to an independent Business Development position. Train yourself to look at the world from a position of abundance rather than scarcity. Learn to trust your understanding of Business Development and your process for developing qualified prospects, and you will find that your effectiveness in your Business Development role will steadily improve.

Psychologically independent Professionals in Business Development have a solid prospecting, qualifying and lead-tracking system that they know they can rely on.

The $6 Million Mind-set
If this concept seems a bit abstract to you, try one of our favorite techniques that we often cover in our workshop. It's called "The $6 Million Mind-set."

Imagine, if you will, that you have $6 million in the bank. Would you likely need your Business Development position? Of course not. You'd be earning well over $250,000 in interest a year. You don't need the job, you simply choose to be in the role. You enjoy Professional Business Development, and it provides an intellectual challenge.

How can the $6 Million Mind-set make a difference in your actions? Consider this example: You're conducting an interview with a prospect. You've asked any number of Bonding and Positioning questions, and you're doing a Diagnostic Interview. The prospect is becoming aware of her pains, concerned about doing something, and is considering a purchase from you. She asks you a tough question: "Why should we consider doing business with you?"

If you are psychologically dependent and desperate to make a sale, you'll jump in with a few predictable, salesperson-type answers, such as, "We've got the best product....We've got the best service...We've got good prices." All are answers that characterize you as psychologically dependent and in need of business.

You understand the application of the principle that your Purpose must come before your Goal.

Now imagine a different scenario. You're on the same call with the same prospect in the same step of your Business Development process. But by some twist of fate, you've acquired $6 million in net worth. You don't need the job in Business Development. You're financially independent and psychologically independent. You simply choose to be in the role you are in. The prospect says, "Why should we consider doing business with you?"

From a psychologically independent position, you are likely to come back with a stronger, more compelling reply. You are more likely to say, "I'm not certain at this point you should. That is ultimately a decision you need to make, but only if it is good for both of us." By being in a state of financial independence, you maintain your psychological independence. You have nothing at stake. You want to do business with the prospect only if it is in her best interest. You understand the application of the principle that your Purpose must come before your Goal. You do not need to sell anything. This is a position of strength that allows you and your prospect to treat each other with mutual respect.

Until you have acquired financial independence, learn to think like you have. Learn the value of developing an efficient, effective prospecting and qualifying system that allows you to keep your funnel full. This will provide the psychological leverage you need in any particular call.

A person with the $6 Million Mind-set knows how to think like a business person, not a salesperson.

Successful Professionals in Business Development are not traditionally good "salespeople." They are master prospectors. A good prospector is never in a dependent position because he or she always knows how to develop additional prospects. A person with the $6 Million Mind-set knows how to think like a business person, not a salesperson. He or she has learned to deal with the emotional limitations of the past and has attained the maturity to work his or her system with a confident mind, trusting the system to provide a positive outcome. With the $6 Million Mind-set, the Business Development Professional is free to pursue prospects on a win/win basis – with the Purpose of serving the prospect and the Goal of financial reward.

10

Financial Decision-Making: Steps 6 and 7

By now you've begun to appreciate the value of having a proactive Business Development System that allows you to disqualify unqualified suspects early. During the first three steps of your system – Homework before the call, Bonding and Positioning, and negotiating Rules Rights and Responsibilities, and communicating Goal and Purpose – you have gathered a wealth of information about your client that made him comfortable in sharing problems with you, if they existed. By completing these first three steps, you prepared yourself for Steps Four and Five, asking permission to interview for pain and completing the Diagnostic Interview.

During your Diagnostic Interview, if done correctly, you have identified an individual or group of individuals who have specific problems that they are aware of and wish to do something about. These could be technical problems, business problems, financial problems or a combination. You have worked these individuals and this opportunity through your pain funnel until they became legitimate prospects. During these steps you may have even shared some information about yourself, your company, your programs and your services – enough information to keep the prospect comfortably assured that you could be able to provide a solution to their problems. At this point you have not discussed the "price" for the

Without fully uncovering the pain and determining the desire to solve it, the discussion of price would be inappropriate.

solution, because without fully uncovering the pain and determining the desire to solve it, the discussion of price would be inappropriate.

Through these first five steps you may have had interviews with a range of individuals, some with more decision-making ability than others. You have gathered some information on the prospect company's financial capability to invest in a solution and who decision-makers may be. It is during Steps 6 and 7 that you confirm this information and set up a contract for presenting the solution. Your Business Development System, although Seven Steps, is actually accomplished in three parts. The first three steps position you to uncover pains, Steps 4 and 5 qualify the prospect, and the third phase qualifies for a presentation. It is appropriate at this time to review what has been done previously to determine that you have a legitimate prospect worth pursuing, and to evaluate information that needs to be confirmed or information that is lacking.

The first three steps position you to uncover pains, Steps 4 and 5 qualify the prospect, and the third phase qualifies for a presentation.

During Steps 6 and 7 of your Business Development process, you will confirm all aspects regarding the financial investment available to solve the problems you have uncovered. You also will determine, and confirm with your prospect, Who will make the purchasing decision, and When and How that decision will be made. In your conversations with your prospect, you have already gathered some information concerning these two areas, but you need to confirm this information in detail before proceeding.

Step 6: Determining the Prospect's Financial Commitment

This is a critical step. If you begin to encounter difficulties here, it is a clear indication that sufficient pain has not been uncovered that the prospect is aware of and motivated to do something about. By now the prospect should be asking you what he should expect to invest to secure a solution to his problem. Discussing too early the cost of a solution without the identification of the pain makes the discussion intellectual and not relevant to the prospect because he has nothing to relate to the investment. It is also important to understand that ultimately only decision-makers can legitimately discuss financial investments. Up to this point, you may have had discussions with a range of individuals about their company's problems, but, chances are, none have the ability to discuss the financial commitment necessary to solving them.

Ultimately only decision-makers can legitimately discuss financial investments.

Once you've established that you have a prospect who has pain, is aware of it and wants to do something about it, you must determine if he has the financial capacity to invest in your solution. If not, one of two things has happened. It is possible that there is no pain to uncover, but it is more likely that you have not yet trained yourself well enough to uncover the pain and bring it to the surface. Our experiences with the individuals that we train have shown that initially they may mistake intellectual interest for pain, and they may be only scratching the surface of the problem. Often, they do not feel comfortable maximizing the effect of the pain as it relates to their prospect personally. This process takes time and cannot be rushed. People who do not have pain naturally will not be interested in investing funds to fix it. On the other hand, individuals who have pain, are aware of it and want to do something about it will find the investment. If your prospect says he or she does not have the financial resources to purchase your solution, return to your earlier steps and double your efforts to understand the business and uncover the problems you can solve.

Individuals who have pain, are aware of it and want to do something about it will find the investment.

Some Professionals in Business Development are reluctant to tackle the financial step because of injunctions from the past that tell them it is impolite to talk about money. It is important to remember that although the individuals within your prospects' companies are affected by the problems, the investment that they make is typically the corporation's money, not their personal money. Your client is not spending his personal money. He is investing the company's money to invest in a solution to problems that affect him and his company. Prospects are more than ready to discuss money, provided they have a problem to relate it to and that you are forthright in bringing it up. From Step 5 of your system on, the question that the prospect will be most interested in is, "How much is this problem going to cost me to solve?" It is important that you respond to the prospect at this time by helping him understand the investment that will be required.

Prospects are more than ready to discuss money, provided they have a problem to relate it to and that you are forthright in bringing it up.

The prospect is receptive to this discussion, provided you use words such as "invest," "budget," "fund" and "allocate." It is important to avoid negative - connotation words such as "cost," "spend," "pay" and "charge." You must be up - front in educating your prospect as to what he must invest to solve his problem. From your previous work and extensive interviews with the prospect to this point, you should easily be able to outline an approximate investment. It is important to tell the prospect that, from your assessment, the solution may require an investment of at least X dollars and should that be a problem, you need to discuss it at this point. Will you disqualify a prospect at this step based on financial availability if sufficient pain has been developed? No. It may require time and discussion to determine how to make the investment, but seldom will the prospect with real pain refuse to seek a solution.

Step 7: Determining Who, When, and How the Decision Will Be Made
There are three critical pieces of information to be determined in this step:

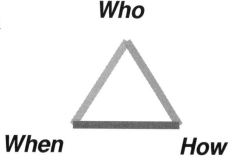

Who

When   **How**

- Who, singularly or as a group, will be involved in the decision-making process?

- When will that decision be made?

- How do the decision-makers go about making their decision?

All three aspects are critically important. If you forget to cover any of these three areas, it will become a problem later, during or after your presentation. By now, with your system, you have talked to a range of people at different decision-making levels. During Step 5, you further qualified decision-makers by understanding that only decision-makers can discuss financial investments. It is important during this step to understand that identifying the decision-maker is only part of the process. You must have a mutual understanding with all decision-makers regarding how and when the decision will be made. As you begin this discussion, you may uncover that there are other individuals involved in this purchasing decision that you had not considered. At this point you may need to restart your system with those individuals and bring them to the point of your other prospects. Delay proceeding into a premature presentation until you have determined who are all the decision-makers, when a decision will likely be made, and how the decision-makers will ultimately come to that decision.

You must have a mutual understanding with all decision-makers regarding how and when the decision will be made.

Remember, only decision- makers can get other people to make decisions. You must have conveyed to the prospect prior to this that you are a decision-maker for your company and in your own personal life. Only such a decision-maker can obtain a decision from other individuals. It is important to understand that you are in no way requiring the prospect to say yes to your company or proposal, but that you are requiring a yes or no decision. If you have communicated your Purpose early in the relationship and established your Goals and discussed the Rules for the Relationship, this step will only be a natural confirmation of what has already been established. You have required the prospect to make multiple decisions to this point in your system. To make a concluding decision of yes or no toward a purchase is the natural next step.

Remember, only decision-makers can get other people to make decisions.

Getting A Business Deal Launched

In many ways, launching a successful Business Development deal is similar to the launching of the space shuttle. Unlikely statement? Maybe not. When NASA sets out to launch the space shuttle, hundreds of experts go through innumerable checklists to confirm that each detail is correct. The shuttle is moved to the launch pad and fueled. From there, the booster rockets will help propel it into space.

In your Business Development process, you are the astronaut delivering a cargo payload consisting of your presentation and solution for the pain of your prospect. To launch your shuttle you need rocket fuel—your prospect's pain – and booster rockets – your prospect's financial commitment and decision-making process. Are these factors identified? Are they sufficiently present? How and when will the decision be made, and by whom?

If the answers to these questions are not clear to both you and your prospect, you are not prepared to launch into a presentation. Remember these two essential Business Development rules: Don't proceed into a presentation until everything is ready, and take a delay rather than launching a premature presentation disaster. The presentation of your business solution is as important to you as the

No one ever listened his or her way out of a sale.

launching of the space shuttle is to NASA. It should be just as meticulously planned. NASA routinely delays flight plans due to the need to double- and triple-check essential details. As a management-level Business Development Professional calling on high-level prospects, you have the same need. Don't attempt to launch into a presentation until every step of your system has been confirmed. Take the necessary time to assure a successful presentation. If you have any doubt, wait until you are sure that your prospect wants a solution to his problem badly enough to do something about it, and wait until you are sure you are dealing with the person or persons who will make the decision about investing the funds necessary to solve the problems. Don't launch your presentation prematurely. Make sure that everyone involved in the purchase is on the same step of your system. Don't take an unnecessary risk by pushing for a presentation when the client doesn't have enough pain, or when there may not be funds available, or when you are dealing with someone who will push hard for a decision but cannot make it himself.

You can never go too slowly in preparing to present. No one ever listened his or her way out of a sale. Your prospect will inform you if there is an immediate need to move forward. Wait for him to do so. Never try to force or rush a conclusion to the deal. When there is a delay, this is your chance to reassess the prospect's pain and desire for resolution, his financial capability and your personal involvement with the decision-making parties.

How and When to Give a Presentation

Long before this point, you have professionally disqualified every prospect except a valid one in a non-threatening, nurturing interviewing process. By this time, your prospect is in a position to make a decision based on your presentation.

In this step, you get to show how you are going to solve the prospect's problem, present the proposal, explain the solution and secure a decision. The prospect has at this point already made a decision to make a decision based on the presentation you present.

The prospect has at this point already made a decision to make a decision based on the presentation you present.

Contrary to what is traditionally taught, the presentation – "showing and telling"- is not the most important aspect of Business Development. The ability to develop qualified prospects is. How valuable is the best presentation if not given to a qualified prospect? If you fail to use your system correctly and make the presentation too early, you are likely to look like you are selling in a traditional manner, and you will meet resistance from your prospect because of his confusion. If you use your system correctly, you will come across as a professional assisting a person in seeking and buying a solution only if it is in his or her best interest to buy it. Your prospect's Purpose will be served ahead of your Goals.

The presentation – "showing and telling" – is not the most important aspect of Business Development. The ability to develop qualified prospects is.

If you have correctly completed your Seven-Step Business Development System to this point, all the momentum is furnished by the prospect. He is forced to qualify as having a problem that he is aware of and seeking to solve before you are required to present a solution. By the time the prospect listens to your presentation, you will have a willing audience prepared to render a decision.

Spend all the time necessary to develop a qualified prospect. Don't try to push a person through your system. Allow that person to work his way through on his own timing and circumstances. If the situation does not reveal a problem you can solve, don't try to force a fit. Simply agree to keep in touch if a problem develops later that you can solve. Don't waste your valuable time making a presentation to someone who doesn't need your product or service.

Spend all the time necessary to develop a qualified prospect. Don't try to push a person through your system.

How to Give a Presentation

Once you have established that you have a qualified prospect with sufficient pain to justify the presentation and that all aspects of the financial commitment and the decision-making process are in place, you are ready for a successful presentation of your company's solution. By waiting until these details are in place, you have created a sense of expectancy and anticipation with your client, who is now favorably inclined to the solution you are about to present. It is important to remember that prospects buy things emotionally from their Child Ego State, but they rationalize the purchase intellectually from their Adult. During your presentation, whether to one person or several, it is important that you address the specific pains that you have uncovered earlier in your process in the priority of importance to the prospect. Address those problems specifically and describe in technical detail how your firm and service will alleviate the concern of the prospect. Concern yourself only with addressing the pain of the prospect. Avoid offering extraneous information that is important to you but not relevant to the prospect. This will only confuse the decision-making process. Presenting too little or too much of an explanation to a

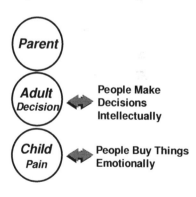

specific pain will also cause a delay and confusion on the part of the prospect making the decision. As you are making a presentation, ask the prospect if what you are presenting makes sense, and relates to and alleviates his concern. Afford him the opportunity to intellectually buy into your solution to their concerns. Taking each concern in the prospect's priority and addressing it in detail allows the prospect to feel comfortable with you, your company and your solution, and will ultimately prepare him for a decision.

Prospects buy things emotion-ally from their Child Ego State, but they rationalize the pur-chase intellectually from their Adult.

Prior to beginning your presentation, you must re-confirm your contract that you will require a decision at its completion. In requiring this decision, it is understood that the prospect has the option of declining the solution. By working your process completely, you will avoid giving free presentations to unqualified people unable to render a decision.

As you complete your presentation, no doubt your adrenaline will be flowing, and both you and your prospect will be looking for a way to mutually complete your process. Your skill in handling your presentation at this point is critical. After answering all questions regarding the prospect's concerns and how you will address them, the appropriate question to ask is "What would you like to do?"

In requiring this decision, it is understood that the prospect has the option of declining the solution.

There should be no pressure felt on either party at this time, only a natural conclusion to a mutually beneficial process. Seldom will you encounter a delay in a decision at this point. If the prospect has been adequately qualified and prepared and the appropriate presentation given, the decision at this point is not "if we do business," but "how we do business." Additional details that may be required to complete the transaction can be handled at this time.

Remember these essentials prior to launching your presentation:

- Don't launch until everything is ready.

- Take a delay rather than launch a disaster.

- Make sure everyone on your system is on the same countdown.

- Don't listen with your motor running, assuming something you want to believe.

- Facilitate the bonding process by establishing a win/win relationship.

- Communicate early that you are a decision-maker requiring a decision, and that it is OK to say no.

If the prospect has been adequately qualified and prepared and the appropriate presentation given, the decision at this point is not "if we do business," but "how we do business."

11

Interviewing and Qualifying Skills

Information/Pain Gathering Techniques

Now that you've developed the thinking and process of a Business Development System, understand how and why people buy, and have a process to qualify and disqualify early, it is necessary to master certain techniques to allow your system to run smoothly. As we consider our 12 Core Competencies of Business Development, we understand the importance of the Four Cornerstones: technical knowledge, business knowledge, people knowledge and money knowledge. We have built on our understanding of Goal-Setting and Planning, having a proactive Business Development System, and now we are prepared to focus on the skills necessary to execute it professionally.

Your ability to master the techniques of Socratic Questioning, Reversing, Nurturing, and acting "dumb" will allow you to secure the necessary information to advance your prospect through your process. By mastering certain basic techniques and skills, you can customize your system to your particular personality. Don't mistake technique for style. Technique is what you do. Style is how you do it. As you learn these interpersonal interviewing skills, remember that all individuals involved in the Business Development process must master them and execute them in harmony when they are involved in joint sales calls.

Don't mistake technique for style. Technique is what you do. Style is how you do it.

Socratic Questioning and the Reversing Process

Socrates, a 5th century B.C. Greek philosopher and teacher, is credited with developing a teaching technique now referred to as Socratic Questioning. This process of questioning allowed his students to develop their knowledge and understanding of a subject. In its simplest terms, Socratic Questioning is the process of asking either intellectual or emotionally based questions to raise an individual's awareness of the subject under consideration. A simpler technique, Reversing, is the process of answering any question with a question. By mastering the art of Socratic Questioning and Reversing, you will be able to maintain control of an interview. Because you are asking the questions, it places the focus on the prospect and allows him to  appear intelligent and in control. It affords you the opportunity to listen rather than talk. It allows the prospect to expand on information he is giving you and go beyond the superficial intellectual answers typically provided. You can then discover his emotionally based pain. Remember this rule: The person who asks the questions is in control of the process, the system and the entire situation.

To begin to employ the Socratic Questioning and Reversing techniques, first learn never to answer a statement. Learn to respond by saying nothing and then asking a question, not making a statement. Next, before responding to a question, make sure you understand why it is being asked. By asking for additional information regarding the question or statement, you will find the underlying motivation or reason for it. This is the information that you need to begin to uncover pain. This is the level you want to reach in the conversation with your prospect.

Socratic Questioning is the process of asking either intellectual or emotionally based questions to raise an individual's awareness of the subject under consideration.

From previous discussions, we have learned that the Child Ego State will generally reveal the pain. Socratic Questioning and Reversing will pull this information from your prospect and move him away from the intellectual atmosphere of the Adult state. Learn to reverse and continue to ask questions until it is completely clear that the prospect is responding from the emotional Child Ego State. This is the posture of the prospect from which you will glean the most useful information.

Generally, you will have to respond with a reversal more than once to get the prospect away from an intellectual Adult discussion to Child-based emotional pain. Don't assume that you understand what the prospect says. Always reverse or question until it is very clear to you exactly what he is expressing. Reversing is a very simple process. The challenge is to stop yourself from answering the prospect's questions or to limit yourself to short answers that will draw out more information. Here are a few examples of simple reversals:

- "Huh?"
- "And?"
- "Oh?"
- "Go on."
- "What?"
- "Tell me more."
- "Help me with…"
- "Which means?"

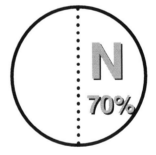

THE NURTURING PARENT

Reversing is an easy technique that develops naturally with practice. But there are two important aspects of this technique you must remember. First, Reversing must always be combined with Nurturing. Otherwise, and rightfully so, it is interpreted as interrogation. Nurturing is simply being supportive. It is personified by the Nurturing Parent part of your personality that we discussed earlier. Remember that you want to move your prospect from the intellectual Adult to the emotional Child Ego State. But when he gets there, you want to be his Nurturing Parent. You want him to feel safe and confident in what he shares. Otherwise, he won't admit his pain. Always precede a reversal with a Nurturing statement. If you don't, your techniques can seem antagonistic. Your prospect may become defensive and respond accordingly. Be sure you've combined Reversing with Nurturing statements such as these examples:

Nurturing is simply being supportive.

- "I understand."
- "Good question."
- "I'm glad you shared that."
- "I sense that's important."

MBD *insights*

Reversing without Nurturing is interrogating.

Another important consideration in connection with the Socratic Questioning and Reversing techniques is knowing when not to use them. If you are asked the same question more than once, do not attempt to avoid the question. Answer it directly. At this point, Reversing could alienate the prospect and cause discord. After the direct answer, you can return to your questioning and Reversing mode. But first, honor the question with an answer.

Practice your Socratic Questioning, Reversing and Nurturing to master your techniques. Try them out in low-risk situations with friends, new acquaintances, at social gatherings or with your colleagues before you try them on your prospect. Always tie a reversal to a Nurturing statement and deliver it in a warm, soft voice. You want to be completely comfortable with these techniques before you employ them in your Business Development process. But don't be uptight about using the Nurturing and Reversing techniques. They work. Most people are self-centered, and they enjoy talking about themselves, their problems and their needs.

MBD *insights*

The person who asks the questions is in control.

MBD *insights*

The key to successful Business Development is getting not giving information.

The Dummy Curve

As a wise man once told his grandson, "There is a limit to how smart you can be, but there's no limit to how dumb you can be." Professionals in Business Development would do well to remember this rule. The Dummy Curve illustrates its wisdom.

Remember when you first went into Business Development? In approaching prospects, you asked a lot of questions, appeared vulnerable and needed help. Consequently, they gave you a lot of information, and tried to be helpful. Typically, your prospect did 80 percent of the talking and most of the work in helping your business deal come together. By actively listening from a vulnerable position, you naturally bonded with your prospects. You were interested in them and in their situation. They qualified themselves, and you stumbled into the business. You felt like a "dummy," but they found reason to buy. At this point in your development, you were unconsciously competent.

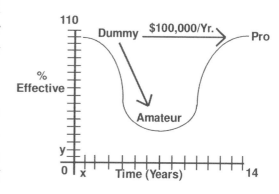

The Dummy Curve

The problem with the unconsciously competent "dummy" is that after finding a few prospects who buy, he begins to think he needs an abundance of product knowledge to improve the process. As he obtains more product knowledge, he feels confident and talks more. Soon he is doing 80 percent of the talking, trying to push the process, and begins to look like a traditional salesperson. The prospect is getting little opportunity to say anything and is feeling intimidated. Our new Business Development Professional now moves from the top left of the Dummy Curve in our chart to the bottom center.

From being an unconsciously competent "dummy," he has learned to be an Amateur. He has learned all the answers, but forgotten all the questions. Chances are he feels more competent and confident. He knows what he's doing. But sales are dropping.

"There is a limit to how smart you can be, but there's no limit to how dumb you can be."

The insightful Professional in Business Development has learned how to be a dummy on purpose. He knows there is a difference between acting dumb and being dumb. He has decided to follow the Dummy Curve back up to the top right position – the Professional.

The Professional knows what he's doing, why he's doing it, why it works. He has decided to look a little "Not OK" on purpose. For a good model of this behavior, watch reruns of the "Columbo" television series. The detective Columbo, played by Peter Falk, never threatens anyone. He acts dumb, and he gathers information from people who never meant to tell him anything. He bumbles, he stumbles, he mumbles statements like these:

- "I don't understand..."

- "Help me. I'm lost..."

- "Am I missing something here...?"

- "Am I out to lunch...?"

"Playing dumb" is a learned skill. You'll be wise to practice it, again in low-risk situations, before you try it on your prospects. The skills of Reversing and playing dumb will provide you more information in the prospecting, qualifying, and lead-tracking process than you would ever have dreamed possible. The time you spend learning these techniques will pay for itself many times over in your growing success in Professional Business Development.

An Amateur has learned all the answers, but forgotten all the questions.

Newton's Laws: Negative Reversing

It might seem at first glance as though there's little relationship between Business Development and the laws of physics. But Professional Business Development people can learn a great deal from the observations of Sir Isaac Newton, the English mathematician and scientist who around 1700 formulated what have come to be known as Newton's Laws. They have sometimes been paraphrased as follows:

There is a difference between acting dumb and being dumb.

170

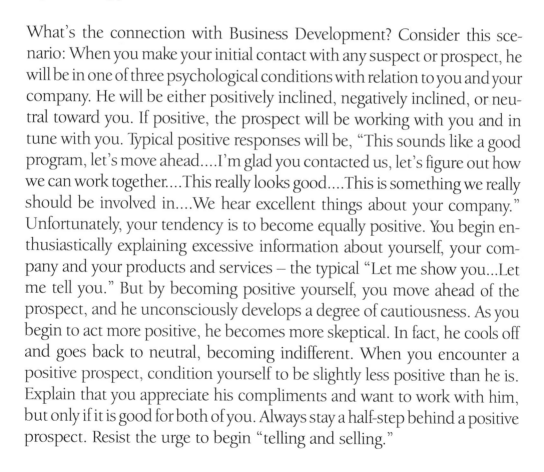

- Law #1 – A body in motion will stay in motion, and a body at rest will stay at rest unless acted upon by an outside force.

- Law #2 – Change in motion is proportional to the force applied.

- Law #3 – For every action, there is an equal and opposite reaction.

What's the connection with Business Development? Consider this scenario: When you make your initial contact with any suspect or prospect, he will be in one of three psychological conditions with relation to you and your company. He will be either positively inclined, negatively inclined, or neutral toward you. If positive, the prospect will be working with you and in tune with you. Typical positive responses will be, "This sounds like a good program, let's move ahead....I'm glad you contacted us, let's figure out how we can work together....This really looks good....This is something we really should be involved in....We hear excellent things about your company." Unfortunately, your tendency is to become equally positive. You begin enthusiastically explaining excessive information about yourself, your company and your products and services – the typical "Let me show you...Let me tell you." But by becoming positive yourself, you move ahead of the prospect, and he unconsciously develops a degree of cautiousness. As you begin to act more positive, he becomes more skeptical. In fact, he cools off and goes back to neutral, becoming indifferent. When you encounter a positive prospect, condition yourself to be slightly less positive than he is. Explain that you appreciate his compliments and want to work with him, but only if it is good for both of you. Always stay a half-step behind a positive prospect. Resist the urge to begin "telling and selling."

What does a negative prospect sound like? He will be hostile, not wanting to see you or hear anything you have to say. A typical response might be, "Why should I be talking to you right now? I'm busy." When you encounter this response, your natural tendency is to begin presenting and defending your position. Remember law #2: Change in motion will be proportional to the force applied. When a prospect goes negative, a traditional salesperson becomes more positive, hoping to push him in that direction. But remember, for every action there is an equal and opposite reaction. In this situation, it is better to go even more negative than your prospect. You might typically say, "Perhaps we shouldn't be talking. It sounds as though this is not an appropriate match. I would be happy to leave if you don't think there is a reason we should be talking." By forcing yourself to go slightly more negative than your prospect, you will give him the space to move toward the neutral and positive positions. At that point, be cautious. Say something like, "I'll be glad to sit and discuss concerns you may or may not have and ways that we can help you if appropriate. But only if you want to. Are you OK with that?"

Neutral prospects are your biggest challenge. While appearing to be open-minded, they are generally uninterested. They typically say things like, "Send me some literature....I'll be glad to look over what you've got....I'll call you.... I'll listen to what you have to say....Give me a presentation, and we'll decide." Your tendency, if you approach the situation from a traditional sales process, is to present, show and tell.

The harder you try to convince a neutral prospect he or she has a problem, the harder the prospect will work to convince you that there is none. Your challenge is to let the prospect convince you that there is a problem. Begin your conversation gently, a bit negatively, and let the prospect work you toward the positive end. If the prospect is neutral, your first task is to get him moving off dead center. If you get him moving toward the negative, the pendulum will soon swing toward the positive. Remember, a body in motion stays in motion. Consider the following exchange as an example:

Charlie, can I have a few minutes to ask you a couple of questions?
Sure, but right now we don't need anything. We're OK.

I understand. I wouldn't want to be presumptuous assuming you do. I'm not sure that right now is necessarily the best time to talk, but I would appreciate the opportunity to ask a couple of questions. Is that OK?
Sure, go ahead.

If someone were to call you and wasn't aware of the problems you had been experiencing and was reluctant to ask about them, what would be the best way to approach you? How would he go about it?
He'd probably ask the question, 'What is your most current problem?'

What would happen then?
We'd probably end up discussing it.

What problem would he be asking you about?
Probably about our problems with on-time shipping. That's the biggest trouble we have right now.

What you're saying to the prospect is, in effect, "I won't pressure you and I won't push you. I'll give you space and allow you to decide whether or not you want to move forward." By taking this approach, you can move a neutral or negative prospect toward the positive reaction you're seeking.

Always stay a half-step behind the prospect and opposite. Negative Reversing is the process of presenting an action or reaction exactly opposite from what is expected. Never try to push or pull. If the prospect asks how you would solve a particular problem, be prepared to say something like, "I will be happy to answer that, but I need to be sure of the problem we are discussing." Allow the prospect to visualize the problem and tell you any additional information you may need before you move to a positive position too quickly.

Negative Reversing is the process of presenting an action or reaction exactly opposite from what is expected.

Of course, if a prospect greets you with a positive reaction that includes a commitment, you don't want to lead him away from that. Simply conclude the business and be thankful for it. But far more frequently you will encounter the neutral or negative prospect, and when you do, be skeptical. Let the prospect prove to you that he needs what you're providing. If your prospect is firmly negative, give him the opportunity to "dump on you." Go even more negative and help the individual dump all negative tendencies. Chances are, that prospect will begin to move toward the positive.

A Professional in Business Development has been trained in techniques well beyond those used by the average individual.

Remember that a Professional in Business Development has been trained in techniques well beyond those used by the average individual. Your Business Development process is in no way based on trying to sell the prospect anything. It allows him to decide for his own reasons what is best for him. Learning to read your prospect and work with him and faithfully execute your system is one of the most powerful techniques you will master.

How to Use Product and Technical Knowledge
With all this talk about asking questions, Reversing and not answering

questions, acting dumb and sometimes being negative, you may begin to wonder if you should even make the effort to learn product and technical knowledge. If you have a good solid technical background, should you simply throw everything you've learned out the window and hope you can stumble, Columbo-like, into a six-figure income?

Yes...and no. You must learn the delicate balance that comes from a thorough understanding of product and technical knowledge that you use only sparingly and with discretion. You need to understand the engineering and technical aspects of your product or service. In your early contacts, your prospects don't care and, chances are, the more you explain it, the more ignorant and Not OK they feel. Instead, you need this knowledge to develop pain questions that will lead your prospect into seeing what your product or service can do for him. And you will need that product knowledge to help give a tailored presentation at the appropriate time.

What problems do you solve for clients? What pains are you able to alleviate? Product and technical knowledge is worthwhile only if you can use it to define problems and solutions.

Product and technical knowledge is worthwhile only if you can use it to define problems and solutions.

A thorough knowledge of the technical aspects of your product or service will assist you in developing a list of "20 Pain Questions" you can ask any prospect at any time. Use your knowledge to focus on the determining factors that qualify prospects as likely clients.

Obviously, as you move toward the presentation of your business solution, your client will have specific technical questions. You need to understand the technical aspects of your product or service to answer these questions credibly. Once you've led the client to understand and deal with the pain your product can solve, you don't want to lose him by appearing ignorant of the basic issues involved.

Don't throw product and technical knowledge out the window. But be careful you don't display it too soon or too frequently simply to dazzle the prospect and make yourself feel OK. Instead, use this knowledge as a foundation for your Diagnostic Interview and a springboard to more effective questions aimed at discovering pain. Then, when you have helped your prospect acknowledge that pain, use your knowledge appropriately to help him see how your product can make his situation better.

Credibility, Confidence and Courage

Credibility, confidence and courage are three interwoven factors that are important for the Professional in Business Development to understand.

> *"For lack of training, they lack knowledge. For lack of knowledge, they lack skill. For lack of skill, they lack confidence. For lack of confidence, they lack victory."*

Julius Caesar is quoted as telling his commander who trained the Roman legions, "For lack of training, they lack knowledge. For lack of knowledge, they lack skill. For lack of skill, they lack confidence. For lack of confidence, they lack victory."

In a crisis, people will do exactly what they have been trained to do. People who are thought to be terribly courageous are more often simply very well trained. What appears to be an intertwined combination of credibility, confidence and courage is often a conditioned response to good training.

It is essential in Professional Business Development, especially at the executive level, to be well trained and able to respond automatically through your training. Until you have become proficient in Professional Business Development, each encounter with a prospect can evolve into a small crisis. As you act on the excellent training you have received, you will begin to possess, in reality and in appearance, credibility, confidence and courage.

First, let's examine credibility, which is of two basic types: immature and mature. Immature credibility is not true credibility at all, but rather an effort to create the appearance of credibility. It surfaces in those with little training in Business Development who, in their effort to hide their fears and Not OKness, plunge forward unequipped to deal with prospects effectively. The immaturely credible waste their own and their prospect's time in an effort to explain why they should be considered credible, i.e., who they are, their capabilities, their company, the features of their products and services, etc.

In a crisis, people will do exactly what they have been trained to do.

Mature, adult credibility, on the other hand, reveals itself through the questions the Professional asks, not through the statements he or she makes. The true Professional has gained the ability to ask questions that convey to the prospect a genuine understanding of his or her world with its attendant challenges and pains. The Professional knows what the prospect's pain looks like and feels like – from the prospect's viewpoint. This real empathy establishes credibility.

Mature credibility reveals itself through the questions the Professional asks, not through the statements he or she makes.

Confidence stems from the successful application of knowledge: knowing what to do, how and when to do it and why it succeeds. Confidence is attained by exploring different techniques in relatively low-risk situations in which failure is not disastrous. From driver training in high school to astronaut training, the procedures involved are learned through a series of repetitions in low-risk situations. Much practice and honing of skills is required before a masterful effort can be made in successful Business Development.

Courage grows from confidence. Confidence grows from learning, practicing and training yourself in the techniques and skills you need in a Business Development interview. When you are confident you will act courageously, and like courageous people in any setting, you will simply do what you are trained to do in the face of real or perceived danger. This will appear, and indeed will be, courageous.

12

The Prospecting Process

The key to your success as a Professional in Business Development is your prospecting and qualifying process. Effective prospecting is as important as effective presenting, for it is the critical first step in selecting the people and companies most likely to need your product or service.

The key to your success as a Professional in Business Development is your prospecting and qualifying process.

By prospecting and qualifying with skill and savvy, you can quickly eliminate those who are "suspects," not prospects, thus saving yourself valuable time, energy and dollars that would be wasted on people who have only an intellectual interest in your product or service. By the time you find yourself face-to-face with a prospect, you will know he has enough pain to be a motivated buyer, and you'll have a good chance of conducting business.

But for most of us, prospecting is also the most difficult first step in Business Development. We shrink from the initial contact, procrastinating as long as possible. Finally we have a talk with ourselves and get pumped up to make the call, only to go limp at the first negative response, even from the prospect's administrative assistant. After the first no, we pace back and forth to the coffee pot, struggling to summon the courage to make the next call.

Why is this? The reasons are twofold. Most of us have both psychological and mechanical barriers to effective prospecting and qualifying. The psychological barriers are far more debilitating, so let's begin with them.

Psychological Barriers to Prospecting and Qualifying

The prospecting and qualifying process is uncomfortable because it places the Professional in Business Development in a vulnerable position. By its very nature, the process involves rejection. The goal is to canvass a number of suspects, seeking a yes-or-no answer. Is this person sufficiently in need of your product or service that he will probably buy it? Yes or no? Obviously, in many cases, the answer will be no. Regardless of the skill or persuasiveness of the Professional in Business Development, the facts of the situation will often dictate a "no."

> *Most of us have both psychological and mechanical barriers to effective prospecting and qualifying.*

Even though we know this intellectually, it's still difficult to receive a negative response without taking it personally. As Professionals in Business Development, we must constantly remind ourselves that the chorus of "no" answers has nothing to do with us personally.

This can be hard on our self-image. Again, the roots of the dilemma can be found in the emotional baggage that most of us have been lugging around since childhood. And again, our Transactional Analysis psychological model can be instructive. To find the source of our discomfort, we need only to look at the Child and Parent Ego States.

The Not OKness Within the Child Ego State

As we learned in our earlier discussion of the Child Ego State, each of us carries within us an insecure, tender, easily wounded Not OK Child. Whenever we are in a particularly vulnerable situation, such as making an initial call, this Not OK Child leaps into consciousness, filling us with insecurities, fears, and the overwhelming conviction that there is something wrong with us. Just let the administrative assistant of your first prospect act officious with you, and your Not OK Child fairly screams, "See? I knew it. What am I doing here? I can't do this."

Injunctions and Attributions from the Parent Ego State

As though the Not OK Child alone were not enough to make prospecting a formidable task, we also have the injunctions and attributions from the Critical Parent Ego State. You remember these: "Don't bother busy people." "Don't play with the phone." "Don't talk to strangers." Their message reinforces the message we're already receiving from the Not OK Child. "Don't bother these people. They're busy. What you have to say is not important. Who do you think you are?"

The combined force of the Not OK Child and the Critical Parent can cause two disturbing emotional states: "Reachback" and "Afterburn."

Together, these burdens of negative emotional baggage can render even the most highly motivated Business Development Professional helpless when faced with the necessity for prospecting. Just when we need the courage to insist on speaking to the CEO, an undermining inner voice reminds us that we are worthless and insignificant.

The combined force of the Not OK Child and the Critical Parent can cause two disturbing emotional states. They're called "Reachback" and "Afterburn," and to the Business Development Professional, they can be debilitating.

Reachback is the situation in which an impending event begins to have an effect on your present behavior. You worry about something that you believe is about to happen. You start thinking, assuming, concluding and fretting, and you soon find yourself in a world that has little if any relationship to reality.

When you're troubled by Reachback, remember this rule: "Worry is interest paid in advance on borrowed trouble."

Reachback is the situation in which an impending event begins to have an effect on your present behavior.

To conquer Reachback, rely on simple, adult planning, and trust your system. When you're tempted to worry, plan. In the prospecting and qualifying context, this means that before making any call, determine exactly what goal you wish to accomplish. What is your plan to reach that goal? Where are you in your prospecting, qualifying and lead-tracking system, and what skills will you use as part of your script to execute that plan with that system? We will discuss understanding the use of a script in detail later in this chapter.

Afterburn can be just as troubling as Reachback. When a past event continues to affect your present behavior, you're experiencing Afterburn. Last week, you called the CEO of Delta Energy Co. He told you in no uncertain terms that he does not talk to outside vendors and suggested you call a junior person in the purchasing department. Today you need to call another CEO, but the Afterburn from last week's experience is simmering in your mind, and you can't pick up the phone.

The solution to Afterburn can be learned as well. The secret is simply to analyze objectively what happened, learn from it, and move on. Don't replay the scenario to yourself, rubbing salt in your wounds. Consider it briefly, figure out what happened, correct it if appropriate and move on to your next challenge.

When a past event continues to affect your present behavior, you're experiencing Afterburn.

The combined effect of Reachback and Afterburn can be deadly. When Reachback and Afterburn overlap, it's called Burnout. You turn into a cinder. You are so worried about the last call and so worried about the next call that you become paralyzed.

Your Greatest Challenge

These outdated, inappropriate attitudes are far more threatening to your success in prospecting and qualifying than any real or perceived lack of skill. Skills and techniques can be learned. That's easy. But the thought patterns caused by lingering emotional baggage must be unlearned. That's much harder.

But it can be done. You can learn to re-program the mental messages from your Not OK Child and your Critical Parent. By continually working on these issues, you can learn to laugh at your emotional baggage. It's OK to make a mistake in Professional Business Development. You won't go from being dumb to being perfect overnight. It will probably take you 700 to 800 hours of active prospecting to become reasonably proficient – probably about a year and a half. During that time, you will unlearn more than you learn. And your unlearning of negative emotional baggage will be the most important determinant of the degree of your success in prospecting and qualifying.

Mechanical Barriers to Prospecting and Qualifying

The importance of the psychological barriers we've just discussed cannot be overstated. But there are other barriers that can seriously hinder your success in Prospecting and Qualifying. These are mechanical barriers – lack of an appropriate process or system, with the associated skills and techniques required to succeed.

The good news about mechanical barriers is that they can easily be overcome. Learning to set a goal before your initial contact, establishing a plan for the attainment of that goal, determining where you are in your prospecting, qualifying and lead-tracking system and choosing the appropriate skills to execute the process are critical to overcoming mechanical barriers. Also critical is the process of building an effective script that you can adapt and become comfortable with in any situation. By doing this you can analyze the effectiveness of the specific skills and techniques you use to execute your process. All of these are easier than unlearning the emotional baggage that we discussed earlier. You can learn to overcome the mechanical barriers in relatively short order.

> *The thought patterns caused by lingering emotional baggage must be unlearned. That's much harder.*

Why a System?

Your first step is to realize the absolute necessity of developing and relying on a script, process and system. Earlier, in Chapter 8, we discussed the reasons why you need a Business Development System. An important part of that system will be your prospecting and qualifying script.

Why do you need a system? Because, remember, if you don't have a system, you are part of someone else's system. They are in control, and you are not. They are pushing your buttons, and you are reacting. By contrast, if you have a system, you have a road map for the prospecting and qualifying process. You know what comes next, and you know what you've missed. A system enables you to structure and focus your behavior, and it allows you to objectively analyze your behavior and the results it yields.

Understanding Your Prospect

In addition to developing and relying on a system, the effective Business Development Professional will learn the value of understanding the prospect. Remember, you cannot know too much about your prospect. Although you may use the technique of asking "dumb" questions as part of your strategy, you must never put yourself in the position of actually being dumb in terms of understanding your prospect.

Before you make the initial call, do your homework. Know the contact's name. Call at the top. Don't hesitate to ask to speak with the president, owner or general manager. Remember, professionals talk with professionals.

Have at least a general knowledge of the product or service the company produces. You don't have to know all the details, but at a minimum you should understand its major markets, competitive forces and basic technology. Whatever you can learn beyond these elementary requirements will aid your understanding of the prospect and hasten the bonding process you hope will take place during your conversations. So, while you don't want to let over-preparation become an excuse for not making the call, don't skimp on this important step either. Learn all you can about the company and the individual you're calling – as quickly and efficiently as possible.

Why Being a Prospect is a Not OK Experience

Being a prospect can be a Not OK experience for the individual you are contacting. By nature, it involves the unpleasant task of accepting that there might be an undesirable situation or problem that requires attention to solve, if it can be solved at all. Also, there is the question of whether or not you and your services can be a resource. All of these uncertainties surrounding the situation can lead to a feeling of Not OKness on the part of the prospect. This, coupled with the fact that 97 percent of people are functioning from some degree of Not OKness most of the time, almost guarantees that your prospect is feeling Not OK. As we discussed earlier in Chapter 4, more often than not an individual with a feeling of Not OKness will choose to alleviate that perception by persuading himself that another is more Not OK than he is. This can wreak havoc for the Business Development Professional. Consider this example. A CEO has a problem that has been avoided, but still won't go away. You have learned of the problem and feel that your company may have a solution. You make the initial contact with the individual to obtain an appointment to discuss the situation.

Unfortunately, when you contact the CEO, you are unaware that he is having a Not OK day. In addition to the Not OKness of the problem and his being in the 97 percent group, there was a spousal conflict at home that morning that resulted in additional feelings of Not OKness. You unknowingly are faced with all of this even before you say hello.

Remember that over-determined behavior – which is overreacting to a situation, or behavior out of context to the situation you are in – is an indication that your Child is hooked and feeling Not OK.

In an effort to feel a bit more OK, the CEO feels it necessary to bring you into a position of more Not OKness than he is experiencing. This can make him reject any efforts on your part to make contact regardless of your purpose and goal. If you are unable to guard against this, you may let yourself slip into a posture of inadequacy based on the CEO's rejection. You could fall into a trap of either bailing out completely or overreacting by beginning a standard sales-type pitch. Remember that over-determined behavior – which is overreacting to a situation, or behavior out of context to the situation you are in – is an indication that your Child is hooked and feeling

Not OK. Faced with the uneasiness of this Not OK posture, you may rush desperately into a "Let me show you..." routine in order to regain your balance.

As you can see, this is a lose/lose scenario based on individual Not OKness. Both of you were hoping to get some of your emotional needs met. The key to avoiding this situation is to make the client feel OK. With experience, training and perception, you can sense right away the emotional state of the client. Instead of retreating into a defensive Not OK position, you could show empathy, stroke the client's ego, and nurture him back into an OK position before you begin your prospecting and qualifying process.

MBD *insights*

Remember that buying is generally a Not OK experience for your client.

Using a Script to Prospect and Qualify

The average length of a prospecting telephone call is approximately 2.5 minutes. It's generally more efficient and effective to make your initial contacts with a prospect by phone. Sixty to 80 percent of your prospecting and qualifying process can be completed by phone, e-mail or fax. Generally, you should avoid calling on prospects face-to-face until you have determined three basic criteria: first, that they have pain you can solve; second, that they are aware of it; third, that they are serious about doing something about it.

Telephone prospecting has several advantages. It's easier to reach more people more quickly. It's easier to track your conversations. And it's easier to "cheat" by phone. You can keep a script in front of you to be sure you ask all the necessary questions in the order you've determined is best. Until you're an old hand at prospecting, you'll find a great deal of security in having a script. If you panic, all you'll have to do is read the next question. Your script will help you "catch" yourself if you have conceptual problems, too. After all, if you have the question written in front of you and you don't ask it, whose problem is it?

Even after you've earned your stripes in Professional Business Development, however, you'll find it easier to use your script in telephone interviews. And most of your prospects will appreciate this efficient method of calling on them. If they don't need your product or service, you haven't wasted their time with a personal interview. If they do need it, you can always agree to a subsequent meeting.

You are a Professional, seeking to do business with other Professionals only when it is mutually beneficial.

At some point, of course, you'll want to meet serious prospects face-to-face. And for each type of interview, you need to be prepared.

For the telephone interview, you need simply to craft your own personal script and have it in front of you. As you interview more and more prospects, you'll continue to refine your script to target more efficiently the information you're seeking. Be sure to include a brief statement of who you are and what your company offers. But remember, you're primarily seeking rather than offering information.

To feel prepared, make sure you're well-acquainted with your script, and remind yourself of some of the helpful concepts we discussed in the Mastering Business Development training, such as the $6 Million Mind-set. Remind yourself that you are a Professional, seeking to do business with other Professionals only when it is mutually beneficial. And remind yourself that if the prospect says "no," that only means you can move more quickly to a more promising prospect.

To prepare for a face-to-face interview, dress the part. Make sure you project a professional, serious image. But be careful not to overdo it. By looking like an ad for Gucci, Rolex or Brooks Brothers, you may intimidate some prospects who are not as fashion-conscious. Remember, your first goal is to make the prospect comfortable. And, since being interviewed in itself can produce some Not OK feelings, be sure your appearance does nothing to deepen your prospect's discomfort.

Another aspect of the face-to-face interview is learning to "play dumb." As we discussed in Chapter 11, by asking questions in the style of the television series "Columbo," you not only can gather much-needed information, but you can allow your prospect to feel OK in the process. And since most people are willing to help a fellow human being who's struggling, you may be more successful in your efforts to lead your prospect into the discovery of a pain-producing problem.

How and Why to Use a Script

Scripting is an integral part of an effective Business Development System. It is an efficient aid for engaging in the initial telephone call. At first, it may appear to be a crutch, but later will prove to be an invaluable aid. It can enable you to classify information obtained through the diagnostic interviewing process. As part of your system, scripting allows you to review, at any point in the interviewing process, any potential problems or positive developments associated with the interview. Scripting is an important organizing component of a Business Development System.

In our Mastering Business Development[2] advanced classes, we discuss the details of writing your script for interviewing prospects. For now, let's look at a few special considerations concerning scripting.

Bonding and Positioning Through Your Script

Bonding is extremely important as part of your Professional Business Development System and should be one of the earliest considerations in developing your script. It can offer you a great deal of knowledge into the probable reaction of your prospect in certain situations. This, therefore, affords you the opportunity to work these situations to your advantage.

Bonding is the step during which you develop kinship with your prospect so that he or she begins to see you not as an outsider, but as a friend who is  sincerely interested in him or her. You move into the prospect's world and the prospect starts to perceive you as "one of us." You want to learn as much as possible about the person, the company and the problems that exist there. To some extent, questions like these will develop naturally as you talk. But don't leave anything to chance. Include in your script a few basic questions to move the process along.

As you gain experience, bonding-related questions will become almost second nature. As you become increasingly relaxed in your developing relationship, bonding becomes simply the natural process of making friends.

As we discussed earlier, bonding is generally accomplished by asking questions about interests, concerns and problems relating to your prospect. These are asked from an emotional or personal standpoint, rather than an intellectual one. Bonding sets the tone for your personal relationship with your prospect and may affect a business relationship profoundly for years.

Goals and Purpose in Your Script

If you are to be a successful Business Development Professional, it is imperative that you set both realistic and meaningful goals. Again, an ingredient of this magnitude must be included in your script. Failure often results from the inability to identify goals. Achievement is, of course, influenced by other factors, but the absence of specific goals almost certainly assures failure.

Your goals in Professional Business Development are short-term, internally focused, and based on "what's in it for me." These include quarterly or yearly targets, your own or your manager's specific measurements of your success.

Your purpose is something much more important. It can be described as "what's in it for someone else." The purpose of any Business Development Professional is to help a client discover what he or she needs or wants – regardless of whether you have it – and to help that client find a way to get it. Remember: If you concentrate on your purpose – to help your clients meet their needs – those clients will help you meet your goals. It's that simple.

As you sketch out your own personal script for interviewing, examine it closely to be sure your questions are client-centered rather than self-centered. Do your questions concentrate on your purpose, as opposed to your goals? If not, edit your script ruthlessly until they do.

Ask yourself, is each step you are taking consistent with that purpose? If the answer is not clear, perhaps it is time to reevaluate your position from both a personal and professional standpoint.

Getting Permission to Ask "Pain Questions"

Interviewing for pain requires permission from the prospect because of the intimate nature and sensitivity of the subject. Admission of company and personal pain is not a comfortable situation outside of a long-standing and trusting relationship. At the "permission point," your bonding process hasn't had time to become entrenched, so you need to ask permission to probe for pain.

Admission of company and personal pain is not a comfortable situation outside of a long-standing and trusting relationship.

There's an important reason why you need permission: No one can fault you for doing what he has given you permission to do. If you've asked your prospect if it's OK to pursue these types of questions, he may or may not answer them honestly. But he won't be offended.

To ensure honest answers to your pain questions, you must move cautiously into this facet of the interviewing process. Preface your questions with requests for permission. For example:

- "Do you feel it would be inappropriate for me to ask...?"
- "If it doesn't make you uncomfortable, may I inquire about...?"

This approach puts the burden of either granting or denying permission on the prospect and, therefore, legitimately places the responsibility at that point. It is also the prospect's option in accordance with the rights of the relationship, which should be in place by this time.

MBD *insights*

No one can fault you for doing what he has given you permission to do.

Scripting Pain Questions

After obtaining permission to probe for pain, you are ready to pursue this line of inquiry. Having done your homework, you should have some idea of the problems (pain) your prospect is facing. Your questioning now needs to be direct, to the point, and concise. This gives the prospect an opportunity to acknowledge pain that you may already suspect and to make you aware of any other areas of concern and the level of willingness to resolve that concern.

A negative tone in questioning at this point is more effective than a positive one. Here are some examples:
- "You probably haven't had to experience..."
- "I doubt that you have ever had a problem like this..."

The negative premise of the question is likely to evoke a more positive response. The assumptive nature of the question almost begs for denial and the chance for the respondent to experience OKness. He's probably thinking, "No, not yet, but we could." You are dealing with double negatives that you will be able to transform into a positive. It is easier for your prospect to admit to pain when your framing of the question prompts that prospect into thinking he or she has taken the lead.

MBD *insights*

A negatively framed question is likely to evoke a positive response.

Searching for No's

Most Business Development Professionals enter their role dreading to hear a prospect say "no." The novice fears nothing more than being turned down.

But as they gain experience and expertise, wise Business Development Professionals learn the value of an early "no." In time, they even seek it out.

Why? Think about it. You approach your role from a professional point of view. Your purpose is quite simply to meet your client's needs, realizing that if you do so, he or she will help you meet your goal of financial success. Either a prospect is interested in your product or service, or he is not. If you're seeking to meet his needs, you're not going to talk him into buying your product or service. Either he needs you or he doesn't. The sooner you find out which type of prospect he is, the more effectively you can use your time to develop Professional Business Development relationships that work for you and your clients. If a prospect is going to be an eventual "no," far better for you if you find that out after one call than after 10 calls and two presentations. Keep this in mind when developing your script, and frame questions that are sufficiently direct and pointed to get an early "no" so you can move on to the next "yes."

Using Your Script to Close

A critical section of your script is the language needed to "close" for the next appointment, to be sure you don't let a top-level prospect slip into "Business Development limbo." This makes it awkward for you to call him back. Have this section of your script handy at every step of your interview.

If at any point you feel your prospect demonstrates sufficient pain and determination to alleviate that pain, go immediately to your closing language. Explain that it seems appropriate to you that the two of you get together in person to talk further. Ask the prospect to set a mutually convenient date, and you have your next appointment set. You're well on your way to a win-win Business Development relationship.

Taking Notes in the Interviewing Process

In a telephone or face-to-face interview, it's important to take notes. Obviously, detailed notes will help you keep at hand the pertinent information about each prospect you interview. When you're making several follow-up calls a week, it's impossible to keep such information in your memory. Make it easy on yourself. Write it down.

There's another equally important reason for taking notes. It makes people feel important. Particularly in a face-to-face interview, your prospect will be a little flattered that you think what he is saying is important enough to be written down. Perhaps unconsciously, he'll appreciate the effort you're willing to invest in the interview, and this appreciation will facilitate the bonding process.

Even if a prospect turns out to be merely a suspect, your notes still have value. Remember, you're going to keep that suspect in your funnel for quite some time. Perhaps today he isn't hurting sufficiently to want to solve his problem. But next year he may be. If you keep your detailed notes and refresh your knowledge of his situation before checking back with him next year, your effort will pay significant rewards.

Personalizing Your Script

You are better qualified than anyone to develop your own personalized script. Spend some time studying the sample scripts provided to you during the Mastering Business Development training, your Mastering Business Development[2] advanced training, and in the Audio Series. But remember, adapt, don't adopt. No script prepared by someone else will be completely right for you. You know your own style and the kinds of questions you will feel comfortable asking. So use these samples only as a guide. You may need to customize your script significantly for different kinds of prospects, but, in general, using the same script will help you become comfortable with the process. The sooner this happens, the better prospector you will be.

Also remember: Your script doesn't have to be perfect. You're involved in a development process. Your script will probably grow and change over time, but no one but you needs to know that. No one but you knows what the script is supposed to accomplish, or even that it is there. And chances are, if you are using any kind of systematic approach, you'll be far ahead of most amateurs who call on your prospect.

No script prepared by someone else will be completely right for you.

Using a script may seem artificial and awkward at first. While you may be comforted by the security it provides, you may also feel somewhat restricted by it. But stick with it until it feels natural to you. Once you've developed and refined your script and lived with it long enough to trust it, you'll find it is an invaluable tool for structuring, tracking and categorizing your prospects. It will be a cornerstone of your Professional Business Development System.

The Next Step

Mastering Business Development® is the first and primary step in our training workshop series designed to install a systematic Business Development Process within your organization.

The next step, Mastering Business Development²®, is the postgraduate workshop series created to help you master the techniques necessary for successful Business Development. Each class in this series of workshops nutures you through the process of developing the concepts and the proactive system essential for becoming a Business Development Professional. It will change not only the way you think, but the way your clients think of you, as you grow beyond the role of supplier to become their valued partner.

Guaranteeing Revenue Results® is the third step in our Business Development Process and focuses on the coaching, counseling, mentoring, and modeling techniques necessary for effective leadership in the Business Development Management role. Through an in-depth process of self-examination, you'll see how to maintain a proactive, results-oriented, focused, and motivated Business Development team. The methods we discuss in this workshop lead to less turnover, higher productivity, and better bottom-line results.

For more information concerning these workshops, contact us at:

Mastering Business Development, Inc. (MBDⁱ)
7422 Carmel Executive Park Dr., Charlotte, NC 28226
(704) 553-0000, (800) 553-7944 FAX (704) 553-0001
Internet: http://www.mbdi.com

Made in the USA
Charleston, SC
27 January 2013